POW!

MY LIFE
IN 40 FEASTS

A COOKBOOK
AND MEMOIR

BY A BELOVED AMERICAN CHEF,
JESSE JONES AND
LINDA WEST ECKHARDT

CHEF JESSE JONES

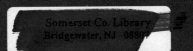

TO: North Plainfield Library

From: Chef Jesse

02-23-2019

Dream big. Nevergiveup. Pow.

Thank you for having me.

Table of Contents

Chapter 12: December — 195

Introduction:

The summer I was four years old, my mother, my sister, and I got on the bus in Newark, New Jersey, and went down South to my grandmother's house in Snow Hill, North Carolina.

I don't remember much about the trip, but when we got off the bus and into a taxi to my grandmother's house, I began to feel uneasy.

Her house was out in the country, a two-and-a-half-room white clapboard house set in the middle of a cornfield. I was afraid of the tall corn stalk trail that led to her house, the noises, the smells, the fact that I couldn't see around it or through it. Where was this trail leading me?

At four years old, this would be my first summer of many, staying down South with my grandmother and grandfather. It all became clear when that cab we came in would leave without me and my sister, with only my mama in the backseat. I could see her crying.

I cried so hard and I thought my life was over. But my grandmother had a way to make things better—with the greatest piece of candy. She gave me a coconut rainbow bar, my all-time favorite. Still love 'em. And it didn't take long for me to see that the love that had come to me from Mama had its roots in my grandmother's house on the farm.

My first lesson that summer came when I got burned on the hot cast-iron stove that sat in the middle of the room. Ouch. That hurt.

But my greatest memory came while helping my grandmother snap green beans. I loved helping her. She would pull up a chair to the table, and I'd stand on it and love everything I saw.

The smells that came out of that little kitchen were amazing. Grandmother was famous for her biscuits and molasses pudding. I tried everything. I loved it all. I was home there at that kitchen table. It's where I belonged.

I created my own molasses cake in honor of my grandmother.

SPICED MOLASSES POUND CAKE

* 3 cups all-purpose flour
* I teaspoon baking powder
* ½ teaspoon salt
* I cup (2 sticks) butter, softened
* I cup dark brown sugar
* I cup granulated sugar
* ½ teaspoon cinnamon
* ½ teaspoon allspice
* ½ teaspoon nutmeg
* 5 large eggs
* 1½ cups molasses
* I cup milk
* I teaspoon vanilla extract
* ½ cup grape-seed oil

— Preheat the oven to 350°F. Combine the flour, baking powder, and salt in a bowl. Set aside.

— In a large bowl, using an electric mixer, cream the butter and sugars together until well mixed, scraping down the sides of the bowl. Beat in the eggs, one at a time. Beating well after each addition, add the flour mixture, alternating with the milk. Mix in the molasses, spices, vanilla and oil. Pour batter into a greased and floured 10-inch Bundt pan and bake for 90 minutes. Cool in the pan for 5 minutes and drizzle with a little molasses.

CHEF JESSE'S SPICE GLAZE

* 1 cup plus 1 tablespoon powdered sugar
* 2 tablespoons evaporated milk
* ¼ cup unsalted butter, softened
* ¼ teaspoon cinnamon
* ¼ teaspoon allspice
* ½ teaspoon pure vanilla extract

— In a medium bowl, add milk and powdered sugar, mixing well. Add softened butter, whip till smooth, and then mix in cinnamon, allspice, and vanilla. Drizzle on cool cake to make a sugar glaze.

Even though that was more than fifty-two years ago, I learned early and surely that the kitchen was where I was meant to be. I loved the sizzling sounds, the smells, the tastes, the love that came from cooking and eating food around that table.

I took a lot of teasing from the men of the family who called me a sissy for staying in there with the women. But I learned right then and there that the kitchen was a safe place and a place filled with joy. I knew it was where I belonged and I've stayed there ever since.

I always feel I have the best of both worlds, with my heart in New Jersey, but girded by the soul of the South!

My first job in a real kitchen came when I was a teenager. I stood in a basement and opened cans. But I could smell those great aromas drifting down from the stove upstairs. I knew I could get there. And I did.

This book tells you about my trip through the kitchens of America. Here are forty feasts that I love and I know you will too. Each feast gives four recipes. You can, of course, add dishes as you see fit. That's what cooking is all about. You start with a good firm foundation and then build your meal just like you'd build a house—item by item. Just know that every recipe in this book has been tested and tasted and is filled with love from the cooks who have gone before you. Welcome to my table.

With love,
Chef Jesse Jones

Acknowledgments

First, I'd like to thank Linda West Eckhardt for helping and believing in me and for being a great co-author.

For my lovely wife, Annette Jones, love you to the moon and back.

My mother, Mildred Jones, thank you for everything. Where would I be without you?

My sister, Priscilla Durant, thank you for casting a positive light on my life.

My friend, Yvonne Durant, thanks for your input in helping us finalize the name of this wonderful book... POW!

Chef Dennis Foy, thanks for giving me an awesome experience in French cuisine.

Thanks to David Verdini, photographer extraordinaire who helped us so much. All photos in the book were taken by David and Chef Jesse.

Thanks, News 12 New Jersey, for allowing me to showcase my talent on TV, along with PIX11 and CBS2 news.

Great towns of South Orange and Maplewood, thanks for keeping me in the spotlight and for hosting events here in my hometown.

Thanks to our inspired editor, Dana Nelson and the extraordinary editorial crew at Outskirts Press who have helped us realize our dream. We are so grateful to you. Outskirts is just the best.

And lastly, but always first in my heart, Avery Thompson, love you forever. Dream big! ... POW!

Foreword

BY JOAN WHITLOW

Two remarkable things about this cookbook reflect what is remarkable about the author, Chef Jesse Jones.

First, you will get what you were looking for when you picked up this book: wonderful food. There is plenty of that. There are feasts to make. And a friendly warmth is infused into the instructions for executing the recipes. As I read, I hear Chef Jesse's big, encouraging, you've-got-this voice cheering you on step by step. I love the fact that he tells you about the special brand of grits he uses for his shrimp and grits—but also makes it clear there is no shame in taking the short route and using instant grits.

There are other recipe books and chefs that get all snooty about a classic French dish like cassoulet. They insist only a certain kind of little white bean will do for this oh-so-French bean and meat stew. Chef Jesse says use black-eyed peas! Cook with what you know and love—nothing wrong with keeping it simple.

But don't be afraid of those little extra steps or trying new combinations that elevate the tried and true into something truly wonderful. That's the other remarkable thing you'll get by diving into Chef's book.

I have eaten his food and loved it. I tried to be a regular patron of his Heart and Soul Restaurant. But I was a reporter who did not work the typical nine-to-five schedule. Too often, by the time I got to Heart and Soul it was closed. Chef Jesse's loyal followers had swooped down like locusts, leaving behind nothing but a menu of what I could have had.

One time I got there just as he was closing. Lamb shanks were all he had left. Most people just want their lamb shanks tender and don't seem to mind if the lamb has been cooked to tasteless mush-meat. Chef Jesse's met the prerequisite for being fork tender. But they also had texture and flavor. The succulent meat was served in a sauce that deserved its own place on the menu. POW!

A few weeks later I had pulled a long drive from my childhood home, Cleveland, Ohio. In the middle of Pennsylvania, I began obsessing about those lamb shanks and whether I could get to Heart and Soul in time. I made it.

"I've got turkey wings," Chef Jesse said. But I wanted lamb shanks. I got a friendly lecture about the concept behind his restaurant. He had certain staple offerings, of course, but the idea was to seek out the freshest, best ingredients each day—farm to table ingredients that would determine that day's menu. So I couldn't count on finding the same items day in and day out.

Chef Jesse was ahead of his time. He was working on a concept that is catching on now. But at the time I wanted lamb shanks, not concepts. I took home the turkey wings. Yes, they were fork tender and so good I didn't bother much with the fork. The turkey wings did not make me forget the lamb shanks. They just added to my obsession for Chef Jesse's cooking.

The other remarkable thing about this cookbook is the way Chef Jesse laces it with his own story. You may be tempted to just get to cookin' and skip the vignettes about his life, the people, and experiences that shaped him. But those stories provide the recipe for the making of this man. And you won't be able to miss even a little taste of Chef Jesse's life. It's a remarkable story.

He grew up in Newark, a city that is most maligned by the people who know the least about it. I won't pretend that Newark's problems are not real: too much poverty, unemployment, and miseducation; too much crime and drugs.

Chef Jesse's story speaks to young people growing up in such cities, growing up with a scream at the edge of their throats, and with anger they don't even understand firing away in their chests. Chef Jesse says he had that kind of anger; he was tempted by the streets.

He tells you how the kitchen, and his love of cooking, saved his life. He was transformed by that love and his drive to succeed as a chef. He was also transformed by the drive to help other people—particularly kids like the one he was.

I have seen that part of him in action. I was an organizer for the 2017 Newark High School Cook-Off, sponsored by the Newark Branch NAACP and Whole Foods, the first competition of its kind in Newark. We carefully chose the chefs, restaurant owners, and caterers we invited to be judges. We wanted people who would inspire Newark's African-American and Hispanic youths about the art and business of cooking. Nobody does that better than Chef Jesse Jones.

He is a big man who leans down to talk to little kids, like the students from his old elementary school, who were at the cook-off serving healthy snacks and smoothies. He was a good, fair, serious judge and leader. It was clear he also came to encourage and to teach students to respect the food, and respect themselves. Chef Jesse's sincere concern that they learn and succeed was a prize that each of the contestants took home that day.

So much of who he is comes through in this book. It is a treasure. Read the book, work the recipes. You will eat well—and feel better about the prospects of cooking up a better world.

Signed,
Joan Whitlow, completely, utterly, and happily retired *Newark Star-Ledger* columnist and editorial board member.

⫸⫷

Chapter 1: January

The great fellowship of family and the special smells that came out of my grandmother's kitchen have sustained me my whole life. I still talk to my mother on the telephone every single day. Family is everything to me. Always has been.

And my relationship to fire started right then and right there. Of course, my grandmother cooked on a potbellied stove and I was fascinated by the process of feeding kindling into that stove, slamming the door shut, and smelling the pungent aroma of smoke and heat that came at me.

She warned me early and often not to touch that stove, not to get too close, and to respect the power that came from that stove. The food that came from it fed us, but one false move and that stove could really hurt you.

Lot of times, I would go out into the yard with Uncle William to cut kindling for that stove and to watch his powerful arms as he raised that hatchet over his head to break that wood into manageable pieces. I found that amazing.

One of my first kitchen jobs was gathering that kindling and taking it to the kitchen, where it was kept in a basket in the corner. I didn't rise from that station for many years.

As a teenager, I got a job back in Newark with a huge operation called Aramark and began my training right at the bottom, literally in the basement. They assigned me to a station where I opened gallon cans and washed dishes. Mountains of dishes. Every single day. I would go home and dream about those dishes and the never-ending stream of cans to be opened.

But one of the major blessings of my life came along about the same time. I met and married my wonderful wife, Annette, who has put up with me for more than 30 years now.

Between the two of us, we earned enough money so we could rent a tiny apartment. Annette has always been good with numbers and she got an office job at Prudential. Life was good.

Our two sons were born during that period. Wonderful Tristan, who was clearly an artist from an early age, sitting on the floor with a box of crayons. Then, a few years later, his brother, whom we call Double J. He was born with a ball in his hands and today, as we speak, is being courted for a spot in the overseas basketball professional leagues. That kid can jump! He simply flies through the air as light as a bird. And he just keeps getting better and better.

And both of our sons earned college degrees. We are proud of that.

God has been good to Annette and me. We try to give back every day. We know we owe a big debt to the universe. We try to pay it forward in every way we can. I try to help others every day. Every day.

But back to the stove.

When I finally got promoted to a station on the line, my real training began. When you work in a large operation like Aramark, you are part of the process of creating restaurant-sized portions of food. This means that some days you might be assigned to make 700 crepes during your shift. Or you might be making gallons of soup. Or you might make 200 sandwiches. It just depends on which slot you're assigned.

But I had an affinity for cooking, a real interest in making it the best that I could, and the patience to do the job, so eventually I rose to the rank of head cook. I have always cared about food. Always.

And the other part of my personality is the piece that says I want to win. I want to make that dish better than anyone has ever made it and I know I can do it.

I am as interested in being the best as a NASCAR driver is in winning the race. Every day. And I'm always like this. I want to win. I want to beat you. I want to make, every day, the best dish that can be made so that the food I make is as good as it can be.

Sometimes, when I'm in a competition it looks like I'm there to beat all the other cooks. But the truth is, I'm there to make my best time, to do my best, to come out ahead, and to know that I did it because I've dedicated my life to this craft, and I'm always in it to win.

This competition cooking actually started in my family, with my aunts and mother and grandmother each trying to best the next one. Fried chicken was a huge part of my growing-up years, and I'm happy to say that now that I've been trained in classical French cooking, my fried chicken is truly the best.

I learned from my grandmother to be my best every day. I also learned another life lesson from her that has sustained me to this day.

"It's not your time," she would say, rocking in her chair. "You have to be patient. Your time will come." And now as you sit here reading this book, I know. My time has come. If only my grandmother were still on this earth to see it.

But I carry her around with me in everything I do, and I offer her to you too. Just read these recipes. Cook them. You, too, will be blessed. That's what cooking can do. It can bring the past forward, and connect you with your own.

Celebrate with a New Year's Day Buffet

✳ Chef Jesse's Black-Eyed Pea Cassoulet with Cornbread Crumb Topping
✳ Harissa Collard Greens
✳ Praline Crusted Old Fashioned Buttermilk Bundt Cake

CHEF JESSE'S BLACK-EYED PEA CASSOULET WITH CORNBREAD CRUMB TOPPING

My first experience with cassoulet was when I walked into Dennis Foy's Town Square Restaurant in Chatham, New Jersey. I was still just a kid and had been working at Aramark, but once I got a whiff of a real French restaurant, I was blown away. The smells were incredible. And that was before I had my first bite. Was I ever in for an education. Thank you, Chef, for three great years in your kitchen.

In the window that first day was a cassoulet ready to be picked up. It was in a big oval French soup tureen, with crusty garlic rosemary toast points.

I made this dish many times under Chef Foy's guidance, but, over the years, as I learned to make the dish, I found I wanted to make it with my spin, adding a bit of my own southern heritage. The first thing I changed were the peas. I believe black-eyed peas make a superior cassoulet, and corn bread on the top? Whooee. Is that good? POW!

Makes 16 servings (can be cut in half)

There are as many cassoulet recipes as there are cooks in rural France. And now I bring my little twist on it to further the cause, as cooks have done forever.

Starting with the iconic black-eyed pea, then using traditional French ingredients and technique, including the D'Artagnan duck leg confit and finishing with a lovely corn bread crumb topping, I make it my own.

The process is long, but not hard. First you soak the black-eyed peas overnight in water. Then rinse and drain.

On the day you're going to serve, get out your biggest stew pot plus a Dutch oven, a sharp knife, and a cutting board, and prepare to be amazed. You're going to sear the meats, one at a time, in the stew pot, then add stock, soaked beans, and diced vegetables. Simmer until beans are soft, about 2 hours.

Build the dish in the Dutch oven by sautéing bacon until crispy; then sauté sausages and duck leg confit* on the whole thing once it's assembled.

Slow cook in the oven until beans are tender and dish is well married. Lift out the duck leg confit and remove the skin and bones. Replace duck meat in the mix and add more stock as needed.

Top with the corn bread crumb topping, pop it back into the oven to finish a few minutes, and then serve. Woowee, the aromas that will float through the house while it's cooking will buckle your knees.

Confit is a traditional method for preserving meat by placing in animal fat to cover. Seals out all air borne bacteria.

Recipe:

- The night before, soak **1½ pounds black-eyed peas** in water to cover. Rinse and drain the next morning

- Meanwhile, sauté **1½ pounds pork shoulder** cut into ¼-inch cubes in a little olive oil in the bottom of the stew pot.

- Make a bouquet garni:

* 2 sprigs fresh parsley
* 2 bay leaves
* 2 whole cloves (or ½ teaspoon ground)
* ½ teaspoon black peppercorns

- Add these into a piece of cotton cheese cloth, tie with kitchen string, then drop the bundle into the stew pot.

- 4 quarts stock (homemade or good quality commercial)

- Soaked black-eyed peas

- Simmer until beans are tender, about 1½ hours, adding stock as needed to keep the level of stock to the top of the beans.

- Then, in a large Dutch oven, heat 1 teaspoon olive oil and sauté **1 pound thick, smoked bacon,** cut into lardons until crispy. Remove to a paper towel to drain.

- Next, brown 1 pound **country sage sausage** (remove casing, then break up in the bottom of the pan). Remove to a dish.

- Brown the vegetables in the bottom of the Dutch oven. As you cut the vegetables add them to the bottom of the pan over medium heat:

* 2 medium yellow onions, peeled and diced
* 2 medium carrots, peeled and diced
* 3 celery stalks with leaves, diced
* 5 garlic cloves, minced fine

- Next, stir **in 2 tablespoons tomato paste** plus sea salt and cracked black pepper to taste and cook about 5 minutes.

- Pour beans and meats on top of the veggies. Top with **4 duck confit**. Cover and let it cook on the stovetop until the duck can be separated from the bones, about 1 hour. Discard skin and bones.

- Chop duck and add it along with everything else back into the pot. Add any necessary stock to cover, then finish in a 275°F oven, or stovetop, covered on simmer.

- Stir from time to time. Cook until vegetables are tender.

- Once the cassoulet is cooked and meltingly tender, add corn bread crumb topping. Run it under the broiler to brown and serve.

CHEF JESSE'S CORNBREAD CRUMB TOPPING

* 1 tablespoon fresh minced garlic
* 2 tablespoons olive oil
* 1 ½ cups Chef Jesse's corn bread, cubed small (make your own—see page 70—or use storebought corn bread)
* Sea salt and cracked black pepper to taste
* 2 tablespoons chopped fresh flat-leaf parsley

- In a medium skillet, cook garlic in oil over low heat about 1 minute, then toss with corn bread, seasonings, and parsley. Stir until crispy and golden brown, about 2 minutes. Sprinkle over cassoulet. Brown and serve.

HARISSA COLLARD GREENS

Harissa is a hot sauce that originated in Tunisia. It lifts flavors and it's so easy to use.

Makes 12 servings

* 2 quarts water
* 2 lbs. smoked turkey wings
* 2 whole onions, peeled
* 2 tablespoons harissa* or to taste
* 4 bunches collard greens
* Sea salt and fresh black pepper to taste

- In a large stockpot, bring water and turkey wings to a boil. Simmer stock, then add onions and harissa. Cook 2 hours, then season to taste with salt and pepper.

- Wash greens in water to cover, remove stems, cut leaves into broad strips and then wash two more times. Drain.

- Remove turkey and onion and chop together. Heat 2 tablespoons olive oil in pot, and sweat the greens until they are limp. Then pour stock back in, adding turkey, onion, and more water to cover as needed.

- Simmer greens in stock about 2 hours, adjusting seasonings to taste.

*Harissa is a Tunisian version of chili paste readily available online at Amazon. Feel free to substitute Jewel hot sauce if you can't find harissa, although I predict if you start using harissa, you'll be hooked.

PRALINE CRUSTED OLD FASHIONED BUTTERMILK BUNDT CAKE

I've made this cake so many times, I could do it in my sleep. It always gets rave reviews and it is easy to make, bake, and eat.

Makes 12-16 servings

- Coat one 10-inch Bundt pan with butter and dust with flour. Set it aside. Preheat the oven to 350°F.

Cake recipe

* I cup unsalted butter
* 2 cups granulated sugar
* 5 large eggs, room temperature
* 3 cups sifted cake flour
* I tablespoon baking powder
* ½ teaspoon kosher salt
* 2 teaspoons vanilla extract
* 1¼ cup buttermilk
* ¼ cup vegetable oil

- In a bowl, sift cake flour, baking powder, and salt.

- In a mixer, cream butter and granulated sugar together. Add eggs, one at a time, beating well after each addition. Stir in dry ingredients alternately with the buttermilk, beginning and ending with flour. Stir in vanilla, then oil.

- **Make the praline** and line into the pans.

* 1½ cups brown sugar
* ½ cup heavy cream
* I tablespoon corn syrup
* ¼ teaspoon kosher salt
* ¼ cup soft butter

* I teaspoon vanilla
* ½ cup chopped pecans

- Combine in a pot and cook and stir for a minute, or until it comes to a boil. Add warm mixture to the bottom of prepared 10" Bundt pan. Pour in the cake batter and spread to mix evenly. Bake 35 to 45 minutes, or until a toothpick comes out clean. Let it stand on a rack 10 minutes, then flip onto a cake plate and cool on a rack. Spread cooling praline over the cake to make a frosting.

Make Martin Luther King Jr's January Birthday a Great Lunch

When January rolls around, it is my honor and duty to acknowledge and remember Dr. Martin Luther King Jr. and his "I Have a Dream" speech. His fight for equal rights in America is my fight as well.

When I think of the civil rights movement, I'm saddened by how things were, but delighted that food played a great part in the decision making of some serious matters, because most meetings were held either around a dinner table where someone was cooking good old southern food, or in a restaurant, where they gathered to talk plans. And as a result, we have a more just and equitable society, one that I leave to my sons with pride.

There is one part of the "I Have a Dream" speech that I practice, live by, and hold dear to my heart.

"I look to a day when people will not **be judged by the color of their skin, but by the content of their character."**

Over the years, I have been treated in the worst way in some kitchens. But as a chef, I have always maintained my integrity and character and worked extremely hard. To make a difference, I learned to respect myself first, then expect the same respect from my peers. Like my grandmother and mother, I try to lead by example. I carry the torch now. Please enjoy my feast and look for my King dinner...POW!

✳ Butternut Squash Soup with Hotcha Honey Shrimp

✳ Spiky Deviled Eggs

✳ Wilted Frisée and Belgian Endive with Radicchio, Bacon and a Spiked Vinaigrette

✳ Winter Pear Tarte Tatin

BUTTERNUT SQUASH SOUP WITH HOTCHA HONEY SHRIMP

This punched-up soup makes a great foil for the spicy shrimp.

Serves 8-12

* 4 tablespoons butter
* I tablespoon grape-seed oil
* I leek, washed and chopped
* 2 garlic cloves, chopped
* I stalk celery, chopped
* I medium carrot, chopped
* 2 medium russet potatoes, peeled and cubed
* I medium butternut squash, peeled, seeded, and chopped
* I quart chicken stock
* Sea salt and freshly ground black pepper to taste
* 2 sprigs fresh thyme, minced
* 2 whole cloves, ground
* 2 whole allspice, ground

— Melt butter and oil in a large stockpot, then add leek, celery, carrot, potato, and squash as you get them prepared. Cook until lightly browned. Pour in stock, add salt, pepper, thyme, cloves and allspice and cover and bring to a boil. Reduce heat to low, cover the pot, and simmer 40 minutes, or until vegetables are tender.

— Transfer the soup to a blender and blend until smooth (or use a stick blender). Return to the pot and add stock as needed to obtain a nice thick mixture. Season with salt and pepper and serve hot.

HOTCHA HONEY SHRIMP

* ½ cup honey
* ⅛ cup diced fresh jalapeño (stems and seeds removed) or to taste
* I pound peeled shrimp – any size

— Season shrimp with sea salt and black pepper. Sauté in a sauté pan with a bit of grape-seed oil. Sear shrimp on both sides until they turn pink. Toss with honey and pepper mixture. Add a spoonful to the top of each soup bowl and finish with minced fresh parsley

SPIKY DEVILED EGGS

Just a whiff of chili powder and hot paprika sprinkled on top of these traditional deviled eggs takes them to a whole new place.

Makes 12

* 6 large hard-cooked eggs, peeled
* I tablespoon Hellmann's mayonnaise
* ½ teaspoon Dijon mustard
* Sea salt and black pepper to taste

— Garnish: sprinkling of chili powder and hot paprika

— Cut eggs in half lengthwise and remove yolks to a small bowl. Mix well with mayo, mustard, salt and pepper. Replace the whites, using a small spoon. Top with sprinkling of chili powder and hot paprika

WILTED FRISÉE AND BELGIAN ENDIVE WITH RADICCHIO, BACON AND A SPIKED VINAIGRETTE

I have loved frisée since my time in the French kitchen. It looks like a light green salad on a bad hair day. Far too wild to be tamed into a neat head, its spiny leaves just go every which way. But the hot and sweet flavor of this French chicory will win you over. The French pair it with buttery bacon cut into lardons. What a good idea. My little twist is to mix it with endive, radicchio, and shallots. Yes.

Makes 8 servings

* 1 small head frisée, cored and cut into bite-size pieces
* 1 head white or red Belgian endive, cored and cut crosswise into strips ½-inch wide
* 1 head radicchio, cored and cut crosswise into strips ½-inch wide
* 3 shallots, minced
* 2 tablespoons chopped fresh chives
* Sea salt and freshly ground pepper, to taste
* 2 tablespoons extra-virgin olive oil
* ½ pound French lardons or other cured, unsmoked bacon, such as pancetta, cut
* into 1/4-inch dice
* 4 tablespoons sherry vinegar
* ½ teaspoon red chili flakes (optional)

– In a large bowl, combine the frisée, endive, radicchio, shallots, and chives. Season with salt and pepper and toss with 2 tablespoons olive oil. Set aside.

– Heat a heavy, nonstick skillet over medium-high heat. Add the bacon and the remaining oil, stirring constantly until the bacon is browned and has rendered much of its fat, about 2 minutes. Add vinegar and cook until syrupy, about 3 minutes. Add optional chili flakes.

– Immediately pour the hot bacon and vinegar over the greens and toss. Serve hot.

WINTER PEAR TARTE TATIN

One of only a few fruits that are actually at their best in the winter, choose Comice or Bosc pears and go forth!

Makes 8 servings

For the pastry dough:
* 2 cups all-purpose flour
* ½ teaspoon kosher salt
* 9 tablespoons chilled unsalted butter
* 6 tablespoons ice water
* 3 tablespoons unsalted butter

For tart:
* ¼ cup granulated sugar
* 3 or 4 firm, ripe winter Bosc or Comice pears, cut in half with seeds scooped out
* (about 2 lb. total), peeled, halved, and cored
* ½ cup firmly packed brown sugar
* 2 tablespoons finely chopped crystallized ginger
* 1 tablespoon fresh lemon juice
* ½ teaspoon ground mace
* ¼ teaspoon EACH: ground cinnamon and cloves

– To make the pastry dough: in a bowl, stir together the flour and salt. Cut the butter into ½-inch chunks and add to the flour mixture. Using a pastry blender or 2 knives, cut in the butter until pea-size pieces form. Add the ice water, 1 tablespoon at a time, stirring lightly with a fork and then rubbing with your fingertips. Gather the dough into a ball, wrap it in plastic wrap, and refrigerate for 15 minutes.

— Preheat an oven to 375°F. Using 1 tablespoon butter, grease a 12-inch round baking dish with 2-inch sides, preferably of glass so you can watch the syrup forming. Sprinkle the granulated sugar evenly over the bottom of the dish.

— Place the pears, cut sides up, in a tightly packed layer in the prepared baking dish. Sprinkle ¼ cup of the brown sugar over the pears. Top with the crystallized ginger and the lemon juice. Cut the remaining butter into bits and dot the tops of the pears. Stir together the remaining ¼ cup brown sugar and the mace, cinnamon, and cloves. Sprinkle the mixture evenly over the pears.

— On a floured work surface, roll out the dough a little larger than the diameter of the baking dish and a scant ¼ inch thick. Drape the pastry over the rolling pin and transfer it to the baking dish. Carefully undrape the pastry over the pears. Tuck the edges of the pastry down to the bottom of the dish to form an interior rim that will encircle the pears once the tart is turned out of the dish. Prick the top all over with a fork.

— Bake until the crust is golden brown, the pears are tender, and a thickened, golden syrup has formed in the dish, about 1 hour.

— Remove from the oven and let stand for 5 minutes. To unmold, run a knife around the inside edge of the baking dish to loosen the sides of the tart. Invert a platter on top of the baking dish and, using pot holders to hold the platter and the baking dish tightly together, flip them. Lift off the baking dish. Serve warm.

Superbowl Sunday Feast

Here's a meal you can eat on your lap while you watch the big game. Just keep that chili hot in a Crockpot or on the back of the stove in a large stew pot. The wings can be made ahead and held in a low oven, and those cookies? POW!

* Chef Jesse's Famous Beef Chili
* Hennessey Chicken Wings
* Red Cabbage and Radicchio Salad with Pecorino
* Garlic Tossed Toasted Pita Triangles
* Giant Chocolate Chip Cookie Pizza

CHEF JESSE'S FAMOUS BEEF CHILI

Who doesn't love chili? Adding a mix of beans gives the dish an added layer of texture and flavor.

Makes 6 to 8 servings

* 1 teaspoon grape-seed oil
* 2 pounds lean ground beef
* 1 cup chopped onions
* ½ cup **EACH**: fresh red and yellow bell peppers
* 4 cloves garlic, chopped
* 1 tablespoon chopped canned chipotle, in adobo sauce
* 3 tablespoons ground cumin
* 3 tablespoons ground chili powder
* 1 cup tomato puree
* 2 cups beef stock
* 1 cup diced fresh plum tomatoes

* 1 cup EACH: pinto beans, kidney beans, pink beans

- Garnish: shredded cheddar, sour cream, and chopped green onions

- In a heavy sauce pot, heat oil to medium and sauté the ground beef meat until brown. Add into a strainer to discard the fat. In the same pot, add back a little oil and sauté onions, peppers, garlic, and chipotle pepper, for 3 minutes. Add cumin and chili powder and tomato puree. Let flavors meld together, and finally, add fresh diced tomatoes, cooked beans, and cook for 30 minutes, stirring from time to time so nothing sticks to the bottom of the pot. Taste and adjust seasonings. Serve in large soup bowls with shredded cheddar, sour cream, and green onions.

- Note: to prepare beans, soak dry beans in cold water overnight, Next day, in a sauce pot, bring water to boil, add 1 small onion, 1 bay leaf, and 1 thyme sprig. Add beans and cook for 2 hours or until fork tender. Reserve for later use.

HENNESSEY CHICKEN WINGS

If you like Buffalo wings, you're gonna love these spicy, sweet wings. POW!

Makes 6-8 servings

* 3 pounds chicken wings
* ⅓ cup Hennessey whiskey
* ¼ cup pepper sauce (any brand)
* 3 tablespoons packed brown sugar

* 4 garlic cloves, minced
* 1 tablespoon grape-seed oil
* 1 teaspoon EACH: fresh squeezed lemon juice, minced tarragon
* ¼ teaspoon crushed red pepper

- Marinate the wings with a mixture of whiskey, pepper, sugar, garlic oil, lemon juice, tarragon, and crushed red pepper in a large bowl. Cover and set aside in the refrigerator overnight. (You can use a Ziploc bag too. Makes it easy to turn the wings from time to time.)

- Heat a grill or oven to 350°F. Lay out wings one layer deep and cook 30 minutes, turning wings once or twice. Serve warm.

RED CABBAGE AND RADICCHIO SALAD WITH GOAT CHEESE AND WALNUTS

Colors, textures, sweet, salty, and nutty. This salad has it all.

Makes 6 to 8 servings

* ½ small red cabbage, finely shredded
* 1 small radicchio, finely shredded
* 2 Belgian endives, finely shredded
* 1 small fennel bulb, fronds reserved and finely shredded
* 2 tablespoons finely chopped flat-leaf parsley
* ½ cup toasted walnuts, roughly chopped
* ¼ cup crumbled goat cheese

For the Dressing:
* 2 tablespoons apple cider vinegar
* 2 tablespoons maple syrup

- * ¼ cup extra-virgin olive oil
- * 2 tablespoons walnut oil
- * sea salt and freshly ground pepper to taste

- Combine the thinly shredded cabbage, radicchio, endive, and fennel in a large bowl with the parsley and chopped fennel fronds.

- Whisk the vinegar, maple syrup, olive oil, and walnut oil in a small bowl. Season with sea salt and freshly ground black pepper to taste.

- Toss the salad with the vinaigrette just before serving. Top with toasted walnuts and crumbled goat cheese. Serve at once.

GARLIC TOSSED TOASTED PITA TRIANGLES

- Quarter pitas and arrange on a baking sheet. Brush with melted butter and garlic. Heat until toasty. Serve at once.

GIANT CHOCOLATE CHIP COOKIE PIZZA

Makes 12 servings

- * 2 cups all-purpose flour
- * 2 teaspoons cornstarch
- * 1 teaspoon baking soda
- * ½ teaspoon sea salt
- * ¾ cup (1½ sticks) unsalted butter, softened to room temperature
- * ¾ cup packed dark brown sugar
- * ¼ cup granulated sugar
- * 1 large egg, at room temperature
- * 2 teaspoons pure vanilla extract

- * 1¼ cup semi-sweet chocolate chips
- * 12-inch pizza pan (one with a lip so there's no spill over the edges)

- Preheat oven to 350°F. Lightly grease a pizza pan with butter. Whisk the flour, cornstarch, baking soda, and salt together in a medium bowl. Set aside.

- Using a hand mixer or a stand mixer fitted with a paddle attachment, cream the butter and both sugars together on medium speed until smooth, about 2 minutes. Add the egg and beat on high until combined, about 1 minute. Scrape down the sides and bottom of the bowl as needed. Add the vanilla extract and mix on high until combined.

- Add the dry ingredients to the wet ingredients and mix on low until combined. With the mixer running on low speed, add the chocolate chips. Dough will be thick and soft.

- Transfer the cookie dough to the pizza pan and flatten out with your fingers or a rubber spatula until the edges reach the sides. Bake until golden, 15-25 minutes..

- Allow the cookie pizza to cool on the pan set on a wire rack before slicing with a pizza cutter. Cover leftovers and store at room temperature for 2-3 days or in the refrigerator for up to 5 days.

Chapter 2: February

Work is work.

I always have kept a little spiral bound notebook and pencil in the breast pocket of my chef's coat. Wherever I am, whatever I am doing, I find it's helpful to jot down what I've learned from the experience of the moment.

Now, of course, I have boxes of these notebooks in a drawer at my house. But not a day goes by that I don't see something that needs to be written down.

*I call it **TAKE NOTE**.*

One way to look at it is to understand that this was the beginning of my culinary training. Just paying attention, making a note, and doing things over and over until they were burned into my brain was the plan.

Whereas the kids today go straight to culinary school, I went straight to work. I made it a practice, and still do, to get to work early, ready to work and ready to go. POW! That's how it started for me, and how it remains today.

I am the first person on the job. I am the last to leave. I come to work clean, suited up, with my notebook in my pocket, and ready to go.

Maybe Chef would tell me to make 700 crepes before the breakfast service began. Let me tell you, do that a few times and make notes and soon you are an expert. It's not rocket science, but it is work. As I tell my students today, "Work is work. Do it over and over until you are fast, accurate, and proud of what you've done." That's how you become a chef.

It's harder for your bosses to disrespect you, to call you names, or to

otherwise humiliate you when you are doing your best, with no attitude except to be a part of the team that gets the job done.

And what is a chef? He's the master of the kitchen, the boss, the leader of all the cooks working under him. That word CHEF gets kicked around a lot now, but it really is quite specific.

Sometimes I think of the line in the kitchen like an orchestra, in which each person is playing their part and in great harmony. Or maybe a dance, where nobody steps on anybody else's feet.

But however you choose to see it, remember that you are a team, working together for one goal: to turn out the best food possible. It's a profession in which I take great pride.

And I've certainly had my struggles with it.

Racism is a fact of life in kitchens. Back when I started, that teamwork would be going great when we were preparing to serve offsite, but often the head of the operation would just tell me and the other black cooks to "lay back" while the others went to serve the food elsewhere.

That was hard to take. Not everybody can hold their temper and just do as they are told in a situation like that. But I had the experiences of my mother and grandmother to draw from, and I'd seen them hold their head up high, keep their dignity, do the best job possible, and draw strength from the act of the work itself, regardless of the indignities that were an inevitable part of life for black and brown people. Then. And now.

⇻⇻⇻✂⇺⇺⇺

Feast of February's Future

* Spiced Shrimp on a Bed of Cheddar Grits Cake
with Haricots Verts

* Cold Oven Pound Cake Dusted with Coconut

Everywhere I ever cooked this spiced-up shrimp dish, people raved. It's beautiful to look at and delicious—one of my trademark dishes. Yes. POW!

SPICED SHRIMP ON A BED OF CHEDDAR GRITS CAKE

Makes 8 servings

* Chef Jesse's spice blend (see below)
* 16 medium shrimp
* ½ cup unsalted butter (1 stick)
* ¼ cup grape-seed oil
* 1½ teaspoon fresh minced garlic
* ½ cup EACH: red and yellow bell peppers
* ½ cup shrimp stock*
* microgreens or fresh minced parsley for garnish

– Remove shrimp from their shells. Keep shells to make a shrimp stock*. Place shrimp in a small bowl, then combine Chef Jesse's seafood spice blend, and mix a couple of tablespoons with the shrimp. Marinate in the fridge for 4 hours or overnight for more flavor—I recommend overnight.

– In a medium sauté pan, melt butter and oil. On medium heat, quickly sauté shrimp on both sides. Remove from pan quickly, using tongs, and set on a plate.

– Sauté garlic and peppers in that same pan for 1 minute. Stirring all the time, add shrimp stock. Let sauce get thick, then adjust seasoning. Add seared shrimp back into the pan and stir to heat shrimp through.

- Serve over cheese grits cakes. Drizzle some sauce on the plate. Finish with microgreens or fresh green herbs.

To make an instant seafood stock, boil shrimp shells in 2 cups hot water with a bit of salt, then strain to make stock. Store up to 3 days covered in the refrigerator.

CHEF JESSE'S SPICE BLEND

Make up a batch of this spice mix except fresh ingredients and keep it in your pantry in a closed glass jar. Add fresh ingredients at the last minute. POW!

* 1 teaspoon dried thyme
* ½ teaspoon EACH: black and white pepper, salt, granulated onion, crushed red pepper
* 1 teaspoon sweet paprika AND granulated garlic

- At serving time add ½ teaspoon EACH: fresh thyme, rosemary, and tarragon, finely minced

CHEF JESSE'S CHEDDAR GRITS CAKES

Makes 24 discs

These POW! flavored discs make a great base for a lot of different dishes. Make up a batch and keep them in the refrigerator until serving time. Then heat them in the oven, plate them, and add toppings. POW!

* 4 cups water
* 1 teaspoon kosher salt

* ½ teaspoon white pepper
* ½ cup butter (1 stick)
* 1 cup old-fashioned or stone-ground grits*
* 1 cup heavy cream
* 1 cup cheddar cheese, shredded
* 1 cup pepper jack cheese, shredded

- Generously butter a 9 x 12 utility pan. Heat water to a boil in a large pot and then add salt, pepper, and butter. Whisk in the grits. Reduce heat to medium, cover, and cook 30 minutes, stirring frequently. Add cream and cook 5 minutes. Stir in cheese, then pour into the prepared pan.

- Cool grits until firm. Use a biscuit cutter to cut them. Arrange on a lightly buttered baking sheet and bake 5 minutes or until tinged lightly brown on the edges.

- To serve, place a grits cake on the dinner plate, top with shrimp, then add a sprinkle of microgreens or parsley.

If you're in a hurry, substitute instant grits and make them following box directions. But for best flavor, use old-fashioned grits, which are sold in grocery stores under the brand Bob's Red Mill.

HARICOTS VERTS WITH SHALLOTS, BUTTER, AND FRESH THYME

Nothing more French than haricots verts. POW!

Makes 8 servings

* 1 pound fresh haricots verts (the French

green bean)

* 2 teaspoons grape-seed oil
* 1 small shallot, minced fine
* 1 teaspoon butter
* 1 teaspoon fresh thyme
* Sea salt and freshly ground black pepper to taste

— Bring a large pot of cold water to a boil. Salt generously and add haricots verts and cook 8-10 minutes, or until tender. Drain and plunge into ice water.

— Heat oil in a large sauté pan over medium heat. Add shallots, butter, and thyme, and cook until shallots are tender, 1-2 minutes. Add beans and toss to coat with the shallot mixture. Taste and adjust seasonings. Serve hot.

COLD OVEN POUND CAKE DUSTED WITH COCONUT

Makes 12-16 servings

Back in the day, when grandmothers made this cake in a wood-burning stove, they measured everything by weight. But now, we measure by volume. Nevertheless, pound cake is one of my standbys. It's easy to make, keeps well, and you can add a lot of different toppings to suit the meal. Or just serve it naked. Yum. Here, we've dusted the cake with simple coconut shreds. POW!

* 3 cups all-purpose flour, sifted
* 1 tablespoon baking powder
* ½ teaspoon sea salt
* 1½ cups unsalted butter
* 2½ cups granulated sugar
* 6 large eggs
* 1½ teaspoons vanilla extract
* ¾ cup heavy cream

— Grease and flour a 10-inch tube or Bundt pan. Do not preheat the oven.

— In a medium bowl, mix flour, baking powder and salt. Set aside.

— In the large bowl of a mixer fitted with the paddle, cream butter and granulated sugar until light and fluffy. Add eggs, one at a time, mixing well each time. Add vanilla.

— Add flour mixture alternately with cream. Beat until smooth. Pour batter into tube or Bundt pan.

— Place cake on the middle rack of a cold oven, set the temperature to 350°F, and bake for 60 to 90 minutes, or until a toothpick inserted into center of cake comes out clean.

— Turn the cake out onto a wire rack to cool. Dust with confectioners' sugar and/or coconut while warm.

— Store in a covered cake plate. Keeps up to a week.

Valentine's Day Is for Lovers

✳ Pecan Crusted Rack of Lamb

✳ Yukon Gold Mash with Truffle Oil

✳ Wilted Garlic Spinach

✳ Double Chocolate Soufflé

My valentine for more than 30 years, Annette, loves me to cook this feast for just the two of us. It's my great pleasure.

PECAN CRUSTED RACK OF LAMB

Makes 2 servings

* 2 lamb racks, cleaned and frenched* (your choice of brand, I prefer Australian)
* 2 tablespoons extra-virgin olive oil
* 2 cloves minced garlic
* 1 tablespoon EACH: fresh minced thyme, rosemary, coarse black pepper, kosher salt
* 2 tablespoons creole mustard
* ¾ cup panko bread crumbs
* ¾ cup toasted chopped pecans

— In a medium bowl, mix oil, garlic, thyme, rosemary, and black pepper together. Rub all over lamb and marinate, covered, in the refrigerator overnight.

Next day:

— Preheat the oven to 425°F.

— Season lamb with kosher salt. In a hot skillet, sear the lamb on both sides for 4 minutes, and until golden brown. Place in a 425°F. oven for 8 minutes, remove from the oven, and let rest.

— Brush meat with creole mustard. Combine crumbs and pecans in a bowl, dredge lamb to cover, and return to oven just to toast for 5 minutes. Serve hot.

How to French a rack of lamb

— Ask your butcher to "French" the rack of lamb. Or, you can do it yourself. Lay the rack on the cutting board, fat side up. Cut away the fat up to the meaty portion, making a clean slice using a sharp knife.

— Flip it over, and using the sharp knife, cut the meaty part away from the bones. Now turn the fatty side UP again and begin slicing the meat away from the fat.

— Pull the fat away from the bone and trim the bones clean with your knife. Now that is a Frenched rack. Wipe the bones clean with a paper towel.

YUKON GOLD MASH WITH TRUFFLE OIL

Makes 6 to 8 servings

* 6-8 medium Yukon gold potatoes, peeled and quartered
* I teaspoon sea salt
* ½ cup butter (½ stick)
* ½ teaspoon freshly ground white pepper
* I cup hot whole milk
* Sea salt to taste
* I tablespoon white truffle oil

— Place peeled and quartered potatoes in a pot of water. Add salt and bring to a boil. Reduce heat to medium and cook for approx. 20 minutes or until cooked through and tender. Drain and mash with potato masher or stick blender. Add butter, hot milk, pepper and salt, and combine. Add truffle oil. Beat well with a stick blender or mixer until fluffy and creamy. Serve hot.

WILTED GARLIC SPINACH

Makes 6 to 8 servings

* ¼ cup grape-seed oil
* 3 cloves garlic, minced
* ½ cup shallots, finely minced
* 4 bunches fresh spinach
* ½ teaspoon EACH: kosher salt and freshly ground black pepper

— Thoroughly wash the spinach and drain in a colander.

— In a large heavy skillet, heat the oil over medium-high heat. Cook and stir garlic and shallots for 2 to 3 minutes; stir in the spinach and cook for 5 minutes. Reduce the heat, stir until wilted, and season with kosher salt, fresh black pepper.

BLACK HAND IN THE POT

One of the big influences when I was cooking with Chef Dennis Foy, always cooking family meals for the staff where we had to use all the leftovers, like the pork backs, was when I first heard of Edna Lewis, who ran Café Nicholas in New York. She changed my life.

I was already doing farm-to-table food. We were already doing Southern, but Edna Lewis showed me how to be authentic. Chef Lewis was from Virginia. She changed the game. She said there were white people in the kitchen with her. It may seem odd to you that this fact made her stand out, but it did.

What I learned from Chef Lewis was how to be true to my roots, to my memories that came through the kitchen door, and to acknowledge and admire the truth of what I learned from my Southern family.

I give you my aunt and my grandmother. It's just a feeling you get through food. It opens up everything in your heart, and you know that though these people are a little intimidating when you start out, if you just stay true to your roots, you'll learn what you need to learn and you'll be free. I'm free now and the kitchen did that for me.

Edna Lewis was the real deal. She always told the stories. She showed people the truth that she was. This really helped me when I was starting out. My whole struggle was: "Am I worthy to work on this line?" And even when it was hard and people were really hard on me, I just smiled. I kept my dignity, my pride, and I just cooked. It has worked for me, just like it worked for Ms. Lewis.

She made this classic French dessert, the chocolate soufflé, famous in America. It was at the time when Julia Child had brought French cooking into American households and when incredible black chefs made it all look easy.

DOUBLE CHOCOLATE SOUFFLÉ

Chef Edna Lewis made her version of this soufflé famous in her New York restaurant, Café Nicholas. In fact, they even put the recipe on the cover of a well-known food magazine of the day.

The big secret is that it's so easy, it will buckle your knees with the first bite.

Makes 10 servings

* 2 tablespoons unsalted butter, plus more for greasing the ramekins
* ½ cup granulated sugar, plus more for dusting
* 6 ounces semi-sweet chocolate, finely chopped
* ¼ teaspoon kosher salt
* ¼ cup whole milk
* 2 tablespoons unsweetened cocoa powder
* 6 large eggs, separated

— Preheat the oven to 400°F. Grease ten 6-ounce ramekins with butter and dust with granulated sugar, tapping out the excess; set on a rimmed baking sheet.

— In a large bowl set over a saucepan of simmering water, melt the semi-sweet chocolate with the 2 tablespoons of butter and the kosher salt, stirring a few times. In another medium saucepan, bring the milk just to a simmer over moderate heat. Whisk in the cocoa powder, and then whisk in the melted chocolate.

— In a large bowl, beat the egg yolks. Gradually whisk in the chocolate mixture until smooth. In another large bowl, using an electric mixer, beat the egg whites at high speed until medium peaks form, about 2 minutes. Gradually beat in the ½ cup of granulated sugar and continue beating until the whites form stiff peaks, 2 to 3 minutes.

— Carefully fold the egg whites into the chocolate mixture until no streaks remain. Spoon the soufflé into the prepared ramekins and bake in the center of the oven until risen, about 15 minutes. Serve right away.

Uncle William's Hunters' Lunch

✳ Uncle William's Rabbit Gumbo with Jasmine Rice

✳ Turnip and Mustard Green Mash

✳ Hush Puppies

✳ Easy Crème Brûlée

UNCLE WILLIAM'S RABBIT GUMBO WITH JASMINE RICE

My uncle William loved grilling rabbit and was a master rabbit catcher in the South when he was a boy. He would set the traps, then check them later. Always exciting.

Uncle William helped me understand where food comes from. It's not just something in the supermarket under a clear plastic wrap. He and all my North Carolina relatives had a serious respect for food and where it came from. They didn't waste a thing and they knew what they were doing. With them, work is work and has real meaning.

Yields 2 quarts

* 3-4 pounds rabbit legs
* I cup Wondra flour + I cup all-purpose flour
* ½ cup grape-seed oil
* ¾ cup **EACH**: onion, green and red bell pepper, medium dice
* ½ cup celery, medium dice
* 2 cloves garlic, minced
* I teaspoon jalapeño, seeded and minced
* I teaspoon oregano, minced
* ½ cup tomato paste
* ½ cup okra, sliced, lightly fried (optional)
* 2 quarts rabbit stock or chicken stock (homemade or store bought)

Feast #6

* 1 cup Andouille sausage (browned in a pan; reserve for later use)
* 1 dash filé* powder

— Dredge rabbit legs in Wondra flour on both sides. In a heavy Dutch oven, heat oil and brown rabbit legs on both sides. Remove and drain on paper towels. Add 1 cup of all-purpose flour to the oil in the pot, and stir slowly to make a peanut butter-colored roux, about 25 minutes.

— Add vegetables one at a time: onions, celery, peppers, garlic, jalapeño, oregano, and sauté until the vegetables are tender. Mix in tomato paste, and continue cooking about 5 minutes. Add fried okra, the stock, and browned sausage. Cook for 45 minutes or more over LOW heat. Taste and adjust seasoning. Add Filè powder, and stir to thicken.

— Serve over Jasmine Rice

Filé (fee-lay) powder is dried sassafras leaves originating in Africa. Available at high-end grocery stores or online. It's a good thickener to keep on hand. It is often used in Cajun and other Southern stews.

TURNIP AND MUSTARD GREEN MASH

Makes 8 servings

* 1 bunch turnips with stems
* 1 bunch mustard greens
* Sea salt and butter to taste
* Water

—

— Bring to a boil a large stew pot of barely salted water. Scrub turnips and add to the pot. Chop greens and add to the pot. Cook until tender. Fish out the turnips and mash them. Pour out most of the water from the pot and add the turnips back to the greens. Season to taste with sea salt and butter. Don't forget to save that pot "likker." Not only is it delicious, but it's loaded with natural vitamins and minerals. POW!

HUSH PUPPIES

Makes about 24

What a quick and easy bread to serve.

* 1 cup yellow corn meal
* ¼ cup all-purpose flour
* 1½ teaspoon baking powder
* ¼ teaspoon sea salt
* ¾ cup milk
* 1 large egg, lightly beaten
* 1 small onion, finely chopped
* 1½ teaspoons grape-seed oil + more to go in the pot for frying

— Combine cornmeal, flour, baking powder, and salt in a medium mixing bowl. Mix well and set aside.

— In another bowl add milk, beaten egg, onion, and oil. Make a well in the middle of the dry ingredients and add wet ingredients, mixing well.

— Heat the grape-seed oil in a deep fryer or a pot with high sides (to avoid splashing hot oil) to 365°F. Use a spoon to scoop the batter, forming oval-shaped hush puppies. Carefully drop the hush puppies into the hot oil, a few at a time. Fry on both sides until golden brown, about 3 minutes. Drain on paper towels. Serve hot.

EASY CRÈME BRÛLÉE

The original French dessert. I figure I made about a jillion of them working for Chef Foy. He taught me such respect for ingredients. Only the best eggs, the best cream, and pure vanilla will do. That and the classic technique will get you there.

Makes 6 servings

* I large egg
* 4 large egg yolks
* ½ cup granulated sugar, plus I tablespoon for each serving
* 3 cups organic heavy cream
* I teaspoon pure vanilla extract
* I tablespoon orange liqueur

– Preheat the oven to 300°F.

– In the bowl of an electric mixer fitted with the paddle attachment, mix the egg, egg yolks, and ½ cup of the granulated sugar together on low speed until just combined. Meanwhile, scald the cream in a small saucepan until it's very hot to the touch but not boiled. With the mixer on low speed, slowly add the cream to the eggs. Add the vanilla and orange liqueur and pour into 6- to 8-ounce ramekins until almost full.

– Place the ramekins in a baking pan and carefully pour boiling water into the pan to come halfway up the sides of the ramekins. Bake for 35 to 40 minutes, until the custards are set when gently shaken. Remove the custards from the water bath, cool to room temperature, and refrigerate, covered with plastic wrap, until firm.

– To serve, spread 1 tablespoon of granulated sugar evenly on the top of each ramekin and heat with a kitchen blowtorch until the granulated sugar caramelizes evenly. Or, place on a baking sheet and run it under the broiler until it bubbles, about 3-5 minutes. Allow to sit at room temperature for a minute until the caramelized granulated sugar hardens.

– PROPANE GAS TORCH SAFETY: Propane gas torches are highly flammable and should be kept away from heat, open flame, and prolonged exposure to sunlight. When lighting a propane gas torch, place the torch on a flat, steady surface, facing away from you. Light the match or lighter and then open the gas valve. Light the gas jet, and blow out the match. Always turn off the burner valve to "finger tight" when finished using the torch.

Chapter 3: March

How the Kitchen Saved Me from the Streets.

I often wonder where would I be without the kitchen. It saved my life.

I grew up in Newark, on High Street. I continued running in the streets. Every day was survival of the fittest. When I walked to school, there were bullies everywhere. I had to learn to fight. But I really wasn't a fighter—just a nice kid who loved to make friends. But that was only inside my heart. On the outside, I had to play tough, act like I wasn't scared. And so I found I could draw on my anger, hit first, and never ask questions later. I could go from zero to 60 in a split second. I grew up with this street anger. It was my weapon, my sword, my salvation. Or so I thought.

When I went to work as a teenager, doing the lowest restaurant jobs there are, I discovered in the kitchen there are all kinds of anger—the chef screaming at the top of his lungs, lots of name calling, fights, and plain old backstabbing. I witnessed it all. For example, one day I had an issue with another cook, and bam, I went at him with a knife. I told him, "I'm from Newark. I don't play." I was serious, but something happened that day that changed my life forever.

Lucky for me, that kid ran away. In a split-second, my life was saved. I looked down at that knife in my hand and knew an important river had been crossed.

From then on, when I would feel anger welling up in me, I would just go to the walk-in, close the door, and scream my lungs out.

No matter how good I was, they treated me like an animal because of my anger. I knew then I couldn't get upset like that, or they would lock me up and throw away the key. I had to control this anger somehow. So I

decided to just smile, no matter what was going on inside.

I became a "yes chef! no chef!" kind of cook, holding all my problems and issues inside. Sometimes I would, as I say, go into the freezer and scream at the top of my voice to get it all out, and then go back to work. I learned to kill them with kindness, and never let them see me sweat. The less information they knew about me, my background, and where I came from, the better for me.

But I was terribly lonely. That's the truth. So, at a young age, I started helping kids who had similar issues; like anger problems, no father, being bullied.

And guess what? When I decided to help kids like that, it helped me conquer my issues as well, giving back, making a difference in young boys' lives. I showed them that they could stay out of jail. My speech has always been, "Let's talk about it, get it off your chest. That's how I controlled my temper. And you can too.""

I had seen my mother and my grandmother always giving and smiling, and I got it. Givers get. It began to work for me. Not only did I find my place at the stove, in the kitchen, but I found a place where I could help others. And when I was focused on others, I began to feel better.

Plus, I just loved to cook—every day, every setting, every opportunity. To focus on the job at hand, to just cook it out, helped make me whole again.

Sometimes, I have to sit down and wonder what happened to that angry young kid who once pulled a knife on somebody. But I know the answer. He went to the kitchen and put that energy to work.

St. Patrick's Day: When we're all Irish for a day

✳ Honey Pineapple Glazed Ham

✳ Braised Savoy Cabbage, Carrots, and New Potatoes

✳ Waldorf Salad

✳ Blondies

HONEY PINEAPPLE GLAZED HAM

Life gets so much easier when you buy a fully cooked spiral sliced ham to start with. To make a ham from scratch see pp 203 for the Christmas ham. POW!

Makes 8 to 10 servings

* 5-pound spiral sliced ham (fully cooked)
* 1 cup pineapple juice
* 1 cup ginger ale
* ¼ cup brown sugar
* ½ cup honey
* 2 teaspoon ground cloves
* 1 fresh orange, juiced, and zest

— Heat oven to 375°F.

— In a medium saucepan, add pineapple juice, ginger ale, brown sugar, honey, cloves and fresh orange juice with zest, and bring it to a hard boil, about 10 minutes. Then pour over the ham in a baking pan. Bake until fully hot, about 20 minutes. Glaze should be semi-thick.

— Serve alongside vegetables and potatoes. POW!

BRAISED SAVOY CABBAGE, CARROTS, AND NEW POTATOES

Makes 6 to 8 servings

To braise means to cook food low and slow so the flavors can marry. My grandmother had a pot on the back of the stove many days to braise whatever she could scare up that day.

* 1 large yellow onion
* 4 medium carrots
* 6 medium red potatoes
* 3 ribs celery, with leaves on top
* 1 Savoy cabbage, about 6 to 8 cups
* 1 tablespoon extra-virgin olive oil
* 2 bay leaves
* ½ teaspoon herbes de provence
* 6 cups chicken stock or water

– Roughly chop onion. Peel carrots; then slice by cutting in half the long way (in 2 or more sections), then into half or quarter circles. Peel and slice potatoes to a similar size. Slice celery, cutting the wide end in half lengthwise. Remove dark green outer leaves from cabbage. Cut off a thick slice, avoiding the core. Lay flat, cut into 3 or 4 wedges, then thickly slice the wedges.

– Heat olive oil in a large soup pot. Add onion and sauté until it starts to get tender, about 5 minutes. Add celery and sauté 5 minutes longer. Add carrots, potatoes, cabbage, herbs, and stock. Cover and simmer until vegetables are tender (30 to 40 minutes).

WALDORF SALAD

Makes 8 to 10 servings

Here's a recipe that was invented in a fancy New York restaurant, but hitch-hiked to the South as soon as it could get there. On every Southern table for holidays.

* 1 large navel orange
* 2 cups diced, unpeeled apple
* 1 teaspoon finely grated orange peel
* ½ cup EACH: raisins, thinly sliced celery, chopped walnuts
* ¼ cup mayonnaise
* 1 tablespoon granulated sugar
* ¼ cup whipping cream
* salad greens or lettuce

– Zest orange for the 1 teaspoon grated orange peel; peel and section orange over a bowl to catch any juices. Cut each orange section in half; reserve 1 tablespoon of the collected orange juice.

– In a large bowl combine diced apple, orange peel, raisins, celery, walnuts, and orange pieces.

– In a separate bowl, blend together mayonnaise, granulated sugar, and reserved orange juice. Fold in cream and gently stir into the apple salad mixture.

– Arrange salad greens on salad plates and top with salad.

BLONDIES

Makes 24 squares

Brownies' cousin, these are rich, easy to make, and easy to eat. POW!

* ½ cup (1 stick) butter, melted
* 1 cup tightly packed dark brown sugar
* ¼ cup molasses
* 1 large egg, lightly beaten
* 1 teaspoon vanilla extract
* ½ teaspoon baking powder
* ⅛ teaspoon baking soda
* Pinch of sea salt
* 1 cup all-purpose flour
* ⅓ cup butterscotch chips
* ½ cup chopped walnuts

— Heat the oven to 375°F. Lightly grease an 8 x 11 inch baking pan with butter.

— In a large mixing bowl, add and stir together melted butter, sugar, molasses, egg, vanilla, then baking powder, soda, salt, and flour. Fold in butterscotch chips and walnuts.

— Lay out onto the baking pan and even it out. Then pop into the oven and bake until golden brown, 15 to 20 minutes. Remove to cooling rack. Cool, then cut into squares. Store in an airtight tin.

March Madness: For Double J, Our Own Basketball Star and Hero

Can I even begin to tell you how proud Annette and I are of our son, Double J? As a recent college graduate, he is being courted by overseas professional basketball. All I can tell you is that he can fly, and when he is on the basketball court, he floats and flies and always gets that ball exactly where he wants it. We are so proud.

This is Double J's favorite celebration dinner after a big game. He is a big guy with a big appetite, and this one does it for Double J.

* Slow-Braised Veal Osso Buco over Parsnip Mash Steamed Garlic Broccoli
* Chef Jesse's Coconut Bread Pudding with Bourbon Sauce

SLOW-BRAISED VEAL OSSO BUCO

(allow one shank per person)

* 4 to 6 veal shanks (12 oz.)
* Chef Jesse's Spice Blend:
* 1 teaspoon kosher salt
* ¼ teaspoon black pepper
* ½ teaspoon white pepper
* 1 teaspoon EACH: granulated garlic, onion, and sweet paprika
* ½ cup grape-seed oil + 2 tablespoons for the pan
* 4 medium carrots, peeled and cut medium dice
* 1 medium onion, cut into medium dice
* 4 celery stalks, cut into medium dice
* ½ cup tomato paste
* 2 cups dry red wine (pinot is great)
* 4 cups beef broth (homemade or store-bought)
* 6 to 8 sprigs fresh thyme

- Preheat the oven to 375°F.

- In a large oven-proof saucepot (or Dutch oven), heat 2 tablespoons oil over medium-high heat until just smoking. Add spice blended shanks and sear on all sides, turning with tongs to get an even golden color. Remove the shanks to a dish and add carrots and onions to the pot. Sauté for 2 minutes, turn once, then add celery, stirring quickly. Add tomato paste, cook for 2 minutes more. Add wine to quickly deglaze the pan.

- Now, stir in the stock, bay leaf, and thyme. Raise the heat to high and bring to a boil, stirring and scraping the bottom. Add shanks back to the saucepot, cover, and place in the oven until tender—about 3 to 3½ hours with oven turned down to 300°. Remove the shanks to a plate. Skim off fat from the pan, bring to a boil, reduce by one-third, and then add shanks back into the sauce. Simmer for 5 to 7 minutes.

PARSNIP MASH

Makes 8 servings

* 8 medium parsnips, scrubbed and cut into large pieces
* Barely salted water to boil
* 1 tablespoon butter
* Sea salt and freshly ground black pepper to taste

- Add parsnips to boiling water and cook until tender, about 15 minutes. Drain, then season with butter, salt and pepper. Mash with a potato masher or stick blender. Serve hot.

STEAMED GARLIC BROCCOLI

Makes 8 servings

* 4 large broccoli heads, stemmed and cut into large pieces
* Large garlic heads, smashed
* Sea salt and freshly milled black pepper

- Place broccoli in a large steamer basket over boiling water. Cover and steam until just tender, about 10 minutes. Remove from the heat, and place in a large serving bowl. In a small pan, melt butter, sauté garlic until it begins to color, then toss with the broccoli. Season to taste with salt and pepper. Serve hot.

CHEF JESSE'S COCONUT BREAD PUDDING WITH BOURBON SAUCE

Bake this old-fashioned dessert in a boiling water bath in the oven. It will be tender and crunchy all at once. POW!

Makes 8 servings

* ½ cup sweetened flaked coconut
* ½ loaf French or white bread
* 6 eggs
* 1 cup granulated sugar
* 1 cup (½ pint heavy cream)
* 2 cups (1 pint) half-and-half cream
* ½ cup dark raisins

* ½ cup golden raisins
* 1 tablespoon almond extract
* 1 tablespoon vanilla extract
* 4 tablespoons unsalted butter

– Preheat oven to 350°F and butter a 2-quart clear baking dish. Toast coconut on a shallow pan until golden brown, about 2 to 5 minutes. Set aside. Trim crust from bread and cut bread into 1-inch cubes. In a large bowl, beat eggs until foamy. Gradually stir in granulated sugar. Stir in heavy cream, half-and-half, and extracts. Soak bread in the egg mixture until moistened. Add coconut and raisins. Mix well. Pour mixture into the baking dish. Place butter over top. Place the baking dish into a baking pan and pour hot water into the pan to a depth of about 1 inch. Bake uncovered for 45 minutes. Serve with your favorite ice cream.

BOURBON SAUCE

Makes 2 cups

* ½ cup (1 stick) unsalted butter, softened
* 3 cups sifted powdered sugar
* ½ cup bourbon

– Beat butter until creamy. Mix in powdered sugar. Mix until light. Add bourbon and pour over warm bread pudding.

Hints of Spring for an Early Easter: Fat Tuesday Begins the Feasting

Signaling the coming Easter, Fat Tuesday is a celebration of festive seasonal foods from the fried oysters to Sweet Potato Soufflé. POW!

Hannah Lewis Jones, a monarch of a woman to me, our Queen of Southern Cooking, from Snow Hill, North Carolina. When I think of my grandmother, food always comes up first, because she was the best; her cakes, pies, and those biscuits. POW!

Losing my grandmother was devastating to our family. She lived to be 92 years old. A godly woman, she trusted in the Lord; her favorite saying was "You better get your soul right for Judgment Day."

I'm very blessed to have experienced my grandmother's teaching, through food and life, the sense of survival that what was served on the table was what you ate— no options or variety. No questions asked. Just clean your plate and say thank you.

So far, up to now, everything she told me has come true. Be humble, help people, and, her favorite line: "Be nice, Junior."

I will continue your legacy and will always bake a pie for you. That's what Hannah did; she made you either a Famous Sweet Potato Pie or Molasses Pudding.

On her birthday, which came on April Fool's Day, 1920, and later when we were all in North Carolina, we would take her to the all-you-can-eat raw oyster buffet that was held every Friday night. She would look that hostess in the eye and say, "Girl, you not making any money tonight, 'cause I'm gonna eat up all those oysters. And then I want a big piece of that sweet potato pie. I hope you learned to make it right, like I taught you."

The proudest moment in my life was when my mom let me deliver the speech at my grandmother's funeral. She died March 15, 2013. Before I approached the stage, I had been listening to folks stand up and say a few words about my grandmother. That moment decided my faith. I knew my purpose in life—my deliverance was to continue her quest to help the sick, the needy, folks who don't have a voice, and, last but not least, the young.

Most in the crowd at her funeral were young people whose lives my grandmother had touched. She lives on inside me, and as she always said, "Don't worry about me, God got me."

God took care of her for 92 years. She didn't suffer or complain—just closed her eyes forever. This is the feast I loved to cook for my grandmother. She loved oysters and here's my little twist on that sweet potato dessert. POW!

* Fried Oysters with Basil Sauce
* Arugula Salad with a Lemon Vinaigrette
* Sweet Potato Soufflé

FRIED OYSTERS WITH BASIL SAUCE

Makes 8 servings

You've heard that you are only supposed to eat oysters in months without an "r" because of those red tides. But cultivated oysters are okay year-round. Serve one or two to each diner, just for an appetizer.

Basil Sauce:
* 1 cup packed fresh basil leaves
* ½ cup extra-virgin olive oil
* Sea salt and freshly milled black pepper

Oyster Breading:
* ½ cup whole milk
* 1 large egg
* 1 cup panko bread crumbs
* 1 tablespoon EACH: chopped chervil, chives, and thyme
* 1 cup all-purpose flour
* 16 large oysters
* Grape-seed oil for frying

- Blanch the basil by bringing a small pan of water to a boil. Add basil and cook only 10-15 seconds. Remove basil to a bowl of ice water to stop the cooking. Lift out of ice water to a strainer and drain. Blot with paper towels.

- Purée basil with olive oil until smooth. Taste and adjust seasoning with salt and pepper. Set aside until serving time.

- Whisk in a small bowl the milk and egg. Set aside.

- Combine in another bowl the bread crumbs with the fresh herbs: chervil, chives, and thyme.

- Place flour on a sheet of parchment and season lightly with salt and pepper.

- Preheat a large frying pan with oil and heat to 375°F.

- Dip oysters first into egg mixture, then give a little shake and place in seasoned flour, coating thoroughly. Shake off excess. Finally, dredge oysters in seasoned bread crumbs and add oysters to the hot oil. Fry 2 minutes or until golden brown. Cool on a paper towel and serve with basil sauce.

ARUGULA SALAD WITH A LEMON VINAIGRETTE

This simple 5-ingredient salad will make your dinner say POW!

Lemon Vinaigrette:
* ¼ cup EACH: freshly squeezed lemon juice and white wine vinegar
* ⅔ cup extra-virgin olive oil
* ½ teaspoon sea salt
* ¼ teaspoon freshly grated black pepper

Salad:
* 8 ounces arugula lettuce
* ¼ cup grated Parmesan
* ¼ cup shaved Parmesan

To make the vinaigrette:
- Place the lemon juice and white wine vinegar in a small bowl and whisk in olive oil to emulsify. Season to taste with salt and pepper.

To make the salad:
- Place the arugula in a large bowl. Pour desired amount of dressing on top and toss to coat. Add grated Parmesan and toss to mix. Add shaved Parmesan to top and serve immediately.

SWEET POTATO SOUFFLÉ

Oh, the competitions between my aunts over this recipe. Who made the best version? Could that one be beat? You tell me. I think mine is best. POW!

* 2 pounds sweet potatoes, scrubbed
* ¼ cup butter, melted
* ¾ cup EACH: white granulated sugar and dark brown sugar
* ½ teaspoon sea salt
* 1 teaspoon vanilla extract
* 1 teaspoon cinnamon
* 3 large eggs
* ½ cup whole milk

- Roast potatoes in a 375°F oven until tender, about 1 hour. Let them cool before peeling.

- Place the potatoes in a large bowl and mash with butter, sugars, salt, vanilla, and cinnamon.

- In a separate bowl, beat eggs until frothy and pour over sweet potatoes along with milk. Whip until light, then transfer to a 9 x 13 baking dish.

- Bake in a 350°F. oven until golden and glistening, about 30 minutes. Serve warm.

- Because there are too many good spring menus to leave any one out, here's our favorite Spring-has-Sprung menu.

Spring Has Sprung Menu

❊ Seared Spiced Salmon Filets

❊ Couscous Pilaf

❊ Polish Paczki (Sugar-Coated Rasberry-Filled Donuts)

SEARED SPICED SALMON FILETS

The early spring vegetables make a perfect bed for salmon

Makes 6 to 8 servings

* 6 to 8 salmon fillets, 6 ounces each
* ½ teaspoon EACH: garlic powder, onion powder, cayenne, sweet paprika, black pepper, and sea salt

– Drizzle olive oil into a medium skillet over medium-high heat.

– In a small bowl, combine spices. Season all sides of salmon filets. Add to skillet when oil is glistening hot.

– Cook for 5-7 minutes on each side, or until a crispy, thin brown outside crust forms and the fish flakes easily when fork-tested. Do not overcook, or salmon will be tough. Transfer to a hot platter. Cover and hold to keep warm.

Meanwhile, make the bed of spring vegetables to form a base for the seared salmon.

* sea salt and freshly ground black pepper, to taste
* 4 oz. snow peas, trimmed
* ⅓ cup fresh peas
* 6 baby carrots with green tops, tops trimmed to 1" and carrots peeled and halved lengthwise
* 1 bunch pencil asparagus secured with a rubber band, trimmed

* ½ teaspoon coriander seeds
* ¼ cup plus I tablespoon extra-virgin olive oil
* 10 cloves garlic, peeled and smashed
* 4 bulbs baby fennel, trimmed and halved, or 2 medium fennel, quartered
* 4 bulbs spring onions, greens thinly sliced; white onions peeled, leaving stem end trimmed and attached, and halved
* 4 cups vegetable stock
* 10 sprigs thyme
* 5 whole black peppercorns
* I bay leaf
* I vanilla bean, split lengthwise
* 3 tablespoons sherry vinegar
* Cilantro sprigs, for garnish
* Crumbled sea salt, for garnish

- Bring a 6-quart saucepan of salted water to a boil. Working in batches, cook snow peas, peas, carrots, and asparagus until crisp-tender, about 1 minute each for peas, and 2–3 minutes for carrots and asparagus. Discard rubber bands from the asparagus. Transfer blanched vegetables to an ice bath until chilled; then drain and set aside.

- Wipe the pan clean and toast coriander seeds over medium-high heat until fragrant, 1–2 minutes. Add $1/_4$ cup oil and cook garlic until golden, 3–4 minutes, and, using a slotted spoon, transfer to a bowl. Cook fennel and white onions until golden, 6–8 minutes; transfer to bowl with garlic. Add sliced onion greens, the stock, thyme, peppercorns, bay leaf, and vanilla bean. Simmer until reduced by half, about 30 minutes. Strain stock and return to pan. Whisk in remaining oil, the vinegar, salt, and pepper, and heat over medium. Stir

in all reserved vegetables. Cook, covered, until vegetables are heated through, 2–3 minutes. Divide vegetables among wide-rimmed soup bowls and ladle broth over the top. Garnish with cilantro sprigs and sea salt. Top with seared salmon filets and a side of couscous.

COUSCOUS PILAF

Couscous originated in Tunisia and other Northern African countries, probably by the Berbers, who learned if they formed millet into little pellets, it cooked better. Now you see couscous made from other grains, including rice and durum wheat. What we buy in the grocery stores today is pre-steamed, easy to cook, and makes a wonderful base for many dishes. But the key to a good couscous is that it should be light and fluffy, never gummy.

* I teaspoon extra-virgin olive oil
* 2 garlic cloves, smashed
* I shallot, minced
* ½ cup whole wheat couscous
* ½ cup chicken broth
* Sea salt and freshly cracked pepper, to taste
* I tablespoon EACH: fresh parsley and chives, chopped

- Heat olive oil in a small saucepan over medium heat, then add the garlic and shallot and cook, stirring constantly, for 2 minutes. Add the couscous and cook, stirring often, for 2 minutes. Add the chicken broth, sea salt, and freshly cracked pepper to taste and bring to a boil. Cover, remove from heat, and let stand for 5 minutes. Add the fresh parsley and chives, then fluff with a fork. Taste and add more seasonings as needed. Serve immediately from a large bowl.

POLISH PACZKI (SUGAR-COATED RASPBERRY-FILLED DONUTS)

Just the thing for the spring feast. I learned to make these at Dennis Foy's restaurant. They were as important to Easter as any other holiday dessert.

Make these as much as 8 hours ahead and let them rest until serving time.

* 2 cups whole milk, warmed to 110°F
* 4½ teaspoons active dry yeast (2 packages)
* ¾ cup granulated sugar, divided
* 5 to 6 cups all-purpose flour, divided
* I large egg
* 4 large egg yolks
* I teaspoon vanilla extract
* I¼ teaspoons sea salt
* 4 tablespoons unsalted butter, melted and cooled
* Grape-seed oil, for frying
* Raspberry or other fruit preserves, for filling

— Powdered and granulated sugars, for coating

— Pour warm milk into bowl of a stand mixer. Stir in the yeast and a pinch of the granulated sugar. Let stand for 5 to 10 minutes, or until it has become bubbly.

Add 2 cups of flour to the mixture and stir with a wooden spoon until a smooth batter forms. Cover with plastic wrap and set in a warm spot for 30 minutes. The mixture rise and be very bubbly.

— In a medium bowl, whisk the egg and egg yolks until pale yellow and frothy, about 3 minutes. Add the remaining sugar, vanilla extract, and salt, and whisk until combined and smooth.

— Attach the dough hook to the mixer. Add the egg mixture to the dough and mix on medium-low speed until mostly combined. Add the melted butter and mix to combine. Gradually add 3 more cups of flour to the mixture and continue to knead until a very soft dough comes together. (It will not clean the sides of the bowl or form a ball. It may be rather slack and a bit sticky.) If necessary, add up to another 1 cup of flour, a spoonful at a time, until a soft dough forms.

— Transfer the dough to a lightly greased bowl, cover with plastic wrap, and set in a warm spot until it has doubled in size.

— Remove the dough from the bowl and turn out onto a floured work surface. With your fingers, smash down the dough into an even layer. Sprinkle flour on the dough and roll it out to ½-inch thickness. If the dough doesn't hold its shape and springs back, cover with a damp towel and let rest for a few minutes and try again.

— Use a 3-inch biscuit cutter to cut out rounds of dough. Transfer the dough rounds to parchment-lined baking sheets. Gather scraps of dough and again roll out and cut until you have used up all the dough. Cover the baking sheets loosely with plastic wrap and place in a warm, draft-free spot until almost doubled in size, about 30 minutes.

— Meanwhile, heat at least 1½ inches of oil in a heavy-bottomed pot or deep skillet over medium heat to 350°F. Place a deep-fry thermometer in the pot and carefully lower about six paczki into the hot oil (be sure not to overcrowd the pan) and fry until the bottom is golden brown. Carefully flip them over and continue to fry until the other side is golden brown. Use a slotted spoon to remove them to a paper towel-lined baking sheet to drain. Allow the oil to come back up to 350°F, then repeat until all of the paczki have been fried.

— Allow the paczki to cool on a parchment sheet until you are able to handle them easily. Using a filling tip, pipe fruit preserves into the sides of the paczki, then roll in powdered sugar. The paczki are best the same day they are made, but can be stored in an airtight container at room temperature for up to 2 days.

The Rise and Fall of my Heart and Soul Restaurant

It was the year 2003, and I was tired of working for people and being treated unfairly, sometimes like I wasn't even a person. So I decided to open my own restaurant and be my own boss.

Well, there's a lot to running the show. You need multiple hats. Just being a great chef is only the beginning. My Heart and Soul restaurant was located on 61 Academy Street, South Orange, New Jersey.

My mission statement was to serve the freshest, free range, and farm-to-table ingredients that I could find. I think I was before my time, because folks then couldn't care less, as long as it was cheap. I was way out ahead of the millennials, who now demand to know every single thing that goes into every dish.

From where I stood in the kitchen, looking out at the dining room, I got at a glance how people perceive Southern cooking. They thought it was all about cheap and inexpensive ingredients.

I went out into the dining room and began talking to my customers. "So why are your prices so high?" These questions were not even very friendly. I could see by the looks on their faces, they thought I was trying to pull a fast one.

So first I tried to convince them. "I'm a trained chef. I have been trained by formally schooled master chefs."

I knew what I was doing, but what I hadn't counted on were the expectations of my customers. The wanted great fresh and natural food so long as it didn't cost them more than mass-produced cheap food. Period.

In the restaurant business, there is a lot of very hard work. Every day it's the same drill; work long hours, go home bone tired, then get up early the next day to go to the fresh foods purveyors to buy the best ingredients to get started and do it all over again.

And there are a million things that can go wrong every day. The sinks can back up. The vendors can get really nasty if you can't pay right on time. Just the ordinary charges for putting the key in the door every morning can be a shock. Electric bill?

You might get a run on fried chicken and run out right at the height of the dinner hour. Or you might buy too much and either have to make a quick change in the menu for the day or put that premium, high-priced fresh bird in the freezer. You can't anticipate everything that gets thrown at you, and you have to make lightning-fast decisions.

Ever wonder where the "Daily Specials" came from? Call it righting the supply and demand problem. It's an ever-present issue in a restaurant, especially one that prides itself on serving the freshest ingredients.

How could I have made more than $200,000 the first year and still be so broke? Money just seemed to fly through my hands. And the wear and tear on the body of a job that requires you be on your feet 15 hours a day—now that was a shock too.

One regret I have is dragging my family into my business. Annette, Tristan, and Jesse hated it, but they helped me and I'm grateful now for them; we are family. But it wasn't their dream, it was mine.

And a restaurant doesn't die a quick and sure death. It takes a long time, more and more sacrifices, until one day you just have to let go. After losing everything, my business, my home, my van—everything and I mean everything!—I knew it was over.

Thank God, my family stayed with me. I will forever be grateful to Annette, Tristan, and Jesse for sticking it out. That was the surest sign of love I ever had.

I had fallen, but I got back up. POW! I dream big and I never give up, but I often sit and ponder. Where did I go wrong? First, you have to maintain your hours. I opened and closed the door based on business, no restaurant walk-ins. I took a catering job and put a sign up on the door, "Be back." You can't do that or you lose the customers who have remained faithful to you. It's one of the hardest lessons to learn about retail. You gotta be open when you say you're gonna be open.

Next the old saying, "location, location, location," knew what it was talking about. Location is very important. Mine wasn't great. Still to date, I hear this from previous owners. What I didn't know then is that 90 percent of new restaurants fail within the first year. And I'm talking the big and the small—those with big bucks behind them and the bootstrap operations. The restaurant business is not for the faint of heart.

Would knowing all this have stopped me from opening Heart and Soul? Probably not. I say Heart and Soul was my graduate school. I learned more in three years there than I could ever have learned in any college.

And the last and hardest lesson I had to learn was when to be convinced you are failing. Not Chef Jesse Jones. I never fail. But maybe that's the key; the ego, the pride, wondering what my chef friends will think.

I didn't want to be a failure, but now I realize you must fail to achieve success. My restaurant lasted for 3 years, and I was out. But on a good note, because my recipes went with me and through my food, I managed to keep the Heart and Soul legacy alive. People still call me up and say, "Jesse, when you gonna open up Heart and Soul again?"

Folks are still talking about my legendary meals. Who remembers my Southern fried catfish, braised oxtails, smothered turkey wings, baby back ribs, BBQ apricot salmon and chicken, supreme roasted chicken, jumbo garlic shrimp, 5-cheese baked mac, candied yams, country potato salad, collard greens and cabbage, stewed green beans, and don't forget my honey buttermilk cornbread!

So where is Heart and Soul?

You are holding it in your hand. All of my recipes are in *40 Feasts*. Heart and Soul will never die as long as good people keep passing the recipes along, cooking and eating and enjoying the feast. Please cook it and remember Heart and Soul restaurant. It's yours now. POW!

April: Yes. March comes in like a lion and goes out like a chicken in the pot. It's April and we're not fooling.

But, I have to tell you, I think it's really true. April is the cruelest month. I always loved it because my beloved grandmother, Hannah Lewis Jones, was born on April Fool's Day. But it's bittersweet to me as well because my grandmother passed away three years ago, and we miss her every day.

But, looking on the bright side, by the time I got old enough to cook for my grandmother Hannah, I started making fried catfish with collards for her on her birthday every year. She would just beam. She loved that feast and loved that I'd make it for her.

And whenever I make she-crab soup, I think of my grandmother, who taught me how to make this gorgeous recipe and taught me about she-crabs in the process.

So, I say to you, whenever you make these April feasts, raise a glass to my beloved grandmother, Hannah Lewis Jones, and to your own grandmother as well. That's what good cooking can do. It can give you a link to your own past whenever you make your grandmother's recipes. And these are two of my favorites from my own beloved grandmother.

Maybe we should call April "Grandmother Month." A good reason to celebrate, don't you think?

Chapter 4: April

The French Connection

* Chef Jesse's Chicken Gumbo
* Carolina Gold Rice Pilaf
* Uber Caesar Salad
* Best Beignets

CHEF JESSE'S CHICKEN GUMBO

Makes 6 – 8 servings

Here's the French connection for sure. Pure French method in this basic Southern gumbo.

* 4 boneless chicken breasts or thighs (6-8 ounces each)
* Chef Jesse's Spice mix:
    * 1 teaspoon EACH: kosher salt, white pepper, fresh thyme and sweet paprika
    * ½ teaspoon EACH: cayenne and black pepper
    * ¼ teaspoon EACH: garlic powder and onion powder
* ½ pound Andouille sausage (browned in a pan, then drained and saved on paper towel)
* 1 cup all-purpose flour
* 1½ cup grape-seed oil + pan drippings
* 1 cup EACH: diced onions, and green and red bell peppers
* ¾ cup chopped celery
* 1 teaspoon minced garlic
* 7 cups chicken stock or water
* 1 teaspoon gumbo filé

- Cut chicken breasts and/or thighs into large pieces. In a medium bowl combine with spice mix and place in a Ziploc bag to marinate overnight in the refrigerator.

- Next day, in a heavy skillet, heat ½ cup oil until hot, then cook chicken – a few pieces at a time – about 2 minutes per side. Remove and drain on paper towels.

- In the same pan, add remaining oil and whisk in flour gradually, cooking to make a red-brown golden roux, about 5 minutes. Remove from the heat and stir in onions, then peppers, celery, and garlic, cooking for 5 more minutes or until vegetables are limp and golden.

- Add stock slowly, bring to a boil, then simmer about a half hour. Taste and adjust seasonings. Add cooked chicken, sausage, and cook about 20 minutes. In the end, sprinkle in gumbo filé. Serve with rice pilaf.

Gumbo filé is a powdered sassafras leaf found in specialty grocery stores or online.

CAROLINA GOLD RICE PILAF

Makes 8 large servings

* ½ teaspoon extra-virgin olive oil
* ¼ cup (½ stick) unsalted butter
* I small onion, finely chopped
* 2 cups Carolina Gold converted rice
* 4 cups chicken stock
* ½ teaspoon EACH: kosher salt and freshly milled white pepper

* I bay leaf
* I sprig thyme

- In a large saucepan, over medium high heat, melt oil and butter. Add onions and cook until transparent, about 3 minutes. Add rice and cook and stir to coat the rice. Once the kernels begin to turn gold, stir in chicken stock, salt and pepper, bay leaf, and thyme. Cover and bring to a boil. Reduce heat and cook about 15 minutes. Turn off heat and let it stand 5 minutes or so.

UBER CAESAR SALAD

You'll make this over and over. So delicious.

Makes 8 to 10 generous servings

Dressing:

* 2 cloves garlic, crushed
* 6 tablespoons grape-seed oil
* ¾ teaspoon kosher salt
* ¼ teaspoon EACH: mustard powder and black pepper
* I½ teaspoons Worcestershire sauce
* ⅛ teaspoon cayenne pepper
* 2 tablespoons fresh lemon juice
* I 2-ounce can anchovy filets
* I large egg
* I French baguette, cut into ½-inch pieces for croutons
* 4 tablespoons melted butter
* I teaspoon Italian seasoning
* ½ teaspoon Worcestershire sauce
* I tablespoon grated Parmigiano Reggiano cheese
* I large head romaine lettuce, rinsed, dried, and torn into bite-size pieces
* ½ cup grated Parmigiano Reggiano cheese

- Preheat oven to 275°F.

- Prepare the dressing in a glass jar by combining the garlic, oil, salt, mustard, pepper, Worcestershire sauce, cayenne, and lemon juice. Rinse anchovy filets under warm water, pat dry on paper towels, and roughly chop. Place anchovy in jar with other ingredients. Cover with tight-fitting lid and shake to mix.

- To coddle the egg, bring 2 inches of water to a boil in a small saucepan. Carefully lower egg in its shell into the water; remove from heat and let it stand for 1 minute. Remove the egg from the water and set aside to cool. Crack open the egg and with a spoon, scrape out all yolk (even the runny white). Use a wire whisk and whip in a small bowl until very frothy. Pour egg into the rest of the dressing and mix well.

- Prepare the croutons by combining the bread cubes, melted butter, Worcestershire sauce, and 1 tablespoon grated cheese. Toss well to coat bread, then place in a single layer on a 10 x 15 jelly roll pan and bake in preheated oven for 20 to 30 minutes.

- Prepare salad in a large bowl by combining the romaine, ½ cup grated cheese, dressing, and croutons to taste. Toss well to coat and serve.

BEST BEIGNETS

Makes about 36 beignets

* I envelope active dry yeast (¼ ounce)
* 3 tablespoons warm water
* ¼ cup whole milk
* ¼ cup shortening
* I teaspoon kosher salt
* I large egg
* 3 cups all-purpose flour
* 4 cups grape-seed oil

- Combine yeast and warm water in a large bowl. Set aside in a draft-free place for 5 minutes to bubble and proof.

- Heat milk in a small saucepan over medium heat. Stir in sugar, shortening, and salt. Remove from the heat and cool to lukewarm, about 100°F.

- Add cooled milk mixture, beaten egg, and 2 cups flour to the yeast mixture. Stir well to combine. Gradually stir in the remaining flour to make a soft dough.

- Turn the dough out onto a lightly floured surface. Knead until the dough is smooth and elastic, about 5 to 8 minutes. Place dough in a well-greased bowl, cover with plastic wrap, and set aside to rise in a warm draft-free place for about 1 hour.

- Preheat a large, heavy pot or Dutch oven. Add oil and heat to 375°F.

- Roll dough on a lightly floured surface to a thickness just under ¼-inch. Cut into 2-½-inch squares. Fry in the hot oil, in batches, so the oil temperature will not dip below 375°F. Fry until golden brown, then cool on paper towels.

- Dust generously with powdered sugar and serve warm.

Southern Fried Feast

✳ Crispy Southern Fried Catfish

✳ Collards with Smoked Turkey Wings

✳ Classic Buttermilk Corn Bread

✳ Grandmother's Sweet Potato Pie

CRISPY SOUTHERN FRIED CATFISH

An electric skillet is ideal for frying because it's so easy to control the heat.

Makes 6 to 8 servings

* 6 to 8 4- to 6-ounce fresh catfish filets

Seafood Spice Blend
* 1 tablespoon sweet paprika
* 2 teaspoons kosher salt
* ½ teaspoon EACH: cayenne pepper, black pepper, white pepper
* 1½ teaspoons granulated garlic and onion
* 1 teaspoon EACH fresh thyme and tarragon, minced

– Combine all ingredients in a small bowl, set aside.

Seasoned Cornmeal Mix
* 1 cup cornmeal (Indian Head)
* ½ cup corn flour (local health food store)
* ½ cup all-purpose flour
* 2 tablespoons of Chef Jesse's spice blend

– Mix together in medium bowl and set aside

Wet mixture

* 1½ cup light buttermilk
* 1 teaspoon or 3 dashes Frank's RedHot sauce to taste
* 1½ inches grape-seed oil for frying in the electric skillet

- In a bowl, add buttermilk, 1 tablespoon of Chef Jesse's blend, and Frank's RedHot sauce. Add catfish, mix well, marinate overnight in a Ziploc bag.

Next-day Prep

- Remove catfish from buttermilk mixture and drain well, shaking excess. Discard buttermilk. In a shallow pan add cornmeal mixture and dredge catfish, coating well. Shake off excess. In an electric fryer or cast-iron pot, heat oil to 365°F.

- Fry catfish, a few pieces at a time, until crispy and starting to float, about 6 to 8 minutes. Drain on paper towel.

COLLARD GREENS WITH SMOKED TURKEY WINGS

Start two to three hours ahead of serving time. Works well to cook the day before and reheat.

Makes 8 servings

* 2 quarts water
* 2 pounds smoked turkey wings
* 2 large onions, peeled and quartered
* ½ teaspoon red pepper flakes
* 4 bunches collard greens, stemmed and thoroughly washed
* 1 medium hot red pepper

* ¼ cup olive oil
* Sea salt and black pepper to taste

- In a large stockpot, bring water and turkey wings to a boil. Add onions and peppers. Reduce heat and simmer 2 hours. Remove turkey meat, onion, and pepper from the pot and set aside.

- In a large pot, heat oil, then sweat the greens about 10 minutes. Season with salt and pepper and red pepper flakes. Pour in the stock. Now add back the turkey, onion, and pepper. Cook an hour or so, or until greens are tender. Serve hot.

- Keeps well, covered in the refrigerator.

CLASSIC BUTTERMILK CORN BREAD IN A BLACK SKILLET

* 1⅓ cups cake flour
* ⅔ cup yellow cornmeal
* ½ cup corn flour
* 1 tablespoons baking powder
* ⅓ cup granulated sugar
* 1¼ cups buttermilk
* ½ teaspoon sea salt
* 6 tablespoons melted butter, divided
* 1 large egg, slightly beaten
* ⅓ cup honey

- Preheat the oven to 350°F. Heat a 10-inch black skillet in the oven.

- Whisk dry ingredients into the wet, taking care not to overmix. Reserve 2 tablespoons of butter to melt in the bottom of the pan.

- Remove hot skillet from the oven. Coat with melted butter, then quickly add the batter. Bake in a hot oven until the center is no longer wet, about 25 to 35 minutes. Check with a wooden skewer or toothpick. Cool on a rack, then cut into wedges and serve.

GRANDMOTHER'S SWEET POTATO PIE

Makes two 9-inch pies

* 2 pounds of sweet potatoes roasted (about 6 large potatoes)
* ½ cup of unsalted butter (softened)
* 3 large eggs, lightly beaten
* ½ cup brown sugar (or to taste)
* 1 teaspoon sea salt
* ½ cup evaporated milk
* ½ cup sweet condensed milk
* 1 teaspoon vanilla extract
* 1 teaspoon allspice
* 1 teaspoon ground cinnamon

– 2 9-inch unbaked pie shells (see pp 134 for recipe) or try those in the red box in the refrigerated section at the grocery stores)

– Place each pie shell into a baking pan. (Tip) I prefer to pre bake the pie shells first for 5 to 7 minutes, be sure to prick the pie shells with a fork so the dough want rise.

– Place sweet potatoes in a 400 degree F oven and roast until tender, about 1 hour.

– Cool then peel and mash with a potato masher, ricer or two forks.

– Set oven to 375 degrees F.

– Combine in a mixing bowl sweet potatoes, butter, beaten eggs, brown sugar, salt, evaporated milk, condensed milk, vanilla, allspice, and cinnamon.

– Beat with a hand mixer or whisk to mix well, and then divide between the two pie shells. Bake 50 to 60 minutes, or until a wooden toothpick comes out clean. Cool and cut into wedges. Great with a dollop of whipped cream on top!

Charleston in a Bowl

* She-Crab Soup: Tart and Tangy Charleston in a Bowl

* Old Bay Biscuits

* Chocolate Soufflé (SEE PAGE 31 FOR RECIPE)

SHE-CRAB SOUP: TART AND TANGY CHARLESTON IN A BOWL

Makes 6 to 8 servings

Order anytime from mid-April to August and use only the best jumbo lump blue crab meat. One of the original Low Country specials of Poor Folks' Cooking. Yum.

* 1 cup unsalted butter
* ½ cup EACH: minced yellow onions and celery
* 2 cloves garlic, smashed
* 1 teaspoon EACH: fresh thyme and tarragon, minced
* 1½ cups all-purpose flour
* 3 cups hot whole milk
* Sea salt and freshly ground black pepper to taste
* Chef Jesse's seafood spice blend to taste (SEE PAGE 26 FOR RECIPE)
* 2 cups heavy cream
* 1 pound jumbo lump blue crab meat
* ¼ cup cream sherry
* Pinch cayenne pepper
* Fresh parsley, chopped for garnish

— Melt butter in a large stewpot over medium heat. Sauté onions, celery, garlic, thyme, and tarragon for about 2 minutes, stirring, until onions are clear.

— Cook and stir in flour and cook a minute or so to make a light roux. Slowly whisk in hot milk, stirring. Add salt and seasonings to taste. Whisk until smooth. Add cream and simmer about 5 minutes. Add crabmeat and cook gently about 25 minutes, barely rippling the surface with bubbles.

— Stir in sherry just before serving. Garnish with chopped parsley.

CHEF JESSE'S OLD BAY CHEDDAR BISCUITS

Makes 20 biscuits

* 4 cups cake flour
* 2 tablespoons baking powder
* I teaspoon baking soda
* I teaspoon sea salt
* ½ cup grated aged cheddar cheese
* ½ teaspoon EACH: thyme, parsley and granulated garlic
* I ¼ cups buttermilk
* I ½ sticks unsalted butter, softened
* I cup shortening (we like Crisco) softened
* ¼ cup of unsalted butter, melted for brushing
* 2 teaspoons Old Bay Seasoning for sprinkling

— Preheat the oven to 425°F.

— In a large bowl, sift together the flour, baking powder, baking soda, and salt. Add the cheese, thyme, parsley, and garlic to the flour mix. Cut in the softened butter and shortening, using two forks, until the mixture resembles coarse meal.

— Combine with buttermilk and stir into the ingredients until moist. Turn out onto a lightly floured surface and knead lightly 3 to 4 times. Do not over-knead. Roll the dough into a rough rectangle about 1 inch thick. Fold over and pat down again. Let the dough rest 10 minutes or so. Pat down again to a 1-inch thick rectangle.

— Cut 2-inch rounds with a biscuit cutter or floured glass, taking care NOT to twist the cutter, then place on a lightly greased or parchment-lined baking sheet. Prick with a fork and brush with melted butter. Sprinkle Old Bay on top, then bake 15 to 20 minutes on 375°F or until lightly browned on top. Cool on a rack. Serve warm.

Crawfish Season Begins with the First Hatch

Although you can't say exactly when crawfish season begins, you'll know it when you see it. Basically, it's when the crawfish begin to hatch, which is when the weather warms up.

* Crawfish Creole with Fluffy White Rice
* Creole Green Beans
* Bread Pudding with Brandy Sauce

CRAWFISH CREOLE WITH FLUFFY WHITE RICE

Makes 8 servings

* 7 tablespoons grape-seed oil
* 4 tablespoons butter
* ½ cup EACH: chopped onions, celery, green and red bell pepper, jalapeño (optional)
* 1 teaspoon EACH: fresh basil, thyme
* 2 cloves smashed garlic
* 1 bay leaf
* 2 teaspoons sea salt
* 2½ teaspoons white pepper
* 1 teaspoon cayenne
* ¼ teaspoon black pepper
* 1 tablespoon dried thyme leaves
* 1½ teaspoons chopped fresh basil
* 3 cups seafood stock (made from boiled shrimp shells and water, strained)
* 2 28-ounce cans peeled tomatoes and juice, chopped
* 1 15-ounce can tomato sauce
* 2 teaspoons granulated sugar
* ½ pound shelled medium shrimp, chopped

* 1½ pounds crawfish, cleaned
* 1½ teaspoons Chef Jesse spice blend (see pp 26)
* ½ teaspoon filé
* 1 cup green onions and tops, chopped

– Heat oil in a large saucepot. Add butter, onion, celery, peppers, and garlic. Cook and stir 3 minutes, or until the onion is clear. Add salt, pepper, cayenne, thyme, basil, and stock. Cook 5 minutes and add tomatoes and granulated sugar. Stir to combine. Raise to a boil. Gently stir in shrimp and crawfish. Remove from heat and let stand 5 minutes. Taste and adjust seasonings with Chef Jesse spice blend and filé. Serve over fluffy white rice made by following box directions. Garnish with green onions and tops.

CREOLE GREEN BEANS

Makes 8 servings

As if green beans were not flavorful enough, punch up the flavor with garlic, shallots, peppers, and tomatoes. POW!

* ½ cup grape-seed oil
* 3 cloves garlic, minced
* 1 cup EACH: minced shallots, red and yellow bell pepper
* 1 jalapeño, seeded, minced (optional)
* 1½ pounds fresh green beans
* 2 plum tomatoes, minced
* ¼ cup tomato juice
* Sea salt and freshly milled black pepper to taste

– In a large skillet, heat oil over medium high heat; then cook garlic, shallots, red and yellow peppers, and jalapeño for about 2 minutes, or until clear.

– Add the green beans and cook and stir about 5 minutes; then add tomatoes and juice, salt and pepper. Serve hot.

BREAD PUDDING WITH BRANDY SAUCE

* 2 cups granulated sugar
* 5 large beaten eggs
* 2 cups whole milk
* 2 teaspoons pure vanilla extract
* 3 cups cubed challah or other eggy bread, allowed to stale overnight in a bowl
* ½ cup packed light brown sugar
* ¼ cup (½ stick) unsalted butter, softened
* 1 cup chopped pecans

For the sauce:
* 1 cup granulated sugar
* ½ cup (1 stick) unsalted butter, melted
* 1 egg, beaten
* 2 teaspoons pure vanilla extract
* ¼ cup brandy

– Preheat the oven to 350°F. Grease a 13 x 9 x 2 inch pan with soft butter.

– Mix granulated sugar, eggs, and milk in a bowl; add vanilla. Pour over cubed bread and let sit for 10 minutes.

– In another bowl, mix and crumble together brown sugar, butter, and pecans.

– Pour bread mixture into the prepared pan. Sprinkle brown sugar mixture over the top and bake for 35 to 45 minutes, or until set. Remove from oven.

For the sauce:

— Mix the granulated sugar, butter, egg, and vanilla in a saucepan over medium heat. Stir together until the sugar is melted. Add the brandy, stirring well. Pour over bread pudding. Serve warm or cold.

Chapter 5: May

This spring, I signed on to help in a local homeless shelter. Yesterday was my first day. It's amazing how every day, you can meet awesome people! God is good. God, please continue to bless IHN, for making a difference in so many people's lives who are homeless and just need some help. I'm so happy to be on board. My mission will always be to feed the hungry.

Time to go Fishing

* Trout Mignonette

* Rutabaga Mash and Braised Ramps

* Mango Sorbet

TROUT MIGNONETTE ON A BED OF RUTABAGA MASH WITH BRAISED RAMPS

Springtime makes me think about fishing. But even if you don't have a ready fishing hole, you're bound to have a great fishmonger to provide you with whole trout come springtime.

Makes 4 servings

* * I cup panko bread crumbs
* * I clove garlic, smashed
* * 2 tablespoons EACH: chopped flat-leaf parsley and oregano leaves
* * Pinch crushed red pepper flakes
* * 3 lemons, juiced plus I lemon, zested and reserved
* * sea salt and freshly milled black pepper to taste
* * ½ cup Dijon mustard
* * 4 10- to 12-ounce trout, boned, belly flap removed, rinsed and patted dry, heads and tails left on
* * Extra-virgin olive oil
* * Mignonette sauce (see below)

– Heat oven to 200°F.

– In a wide, flat dish, combine bread crumbs, garlic, parsley, oregano, red pepper flakes, and zest of 1 lemon, with salt and pepper to taste.

– In a small bowl, mix the mustard and the juice of 1 lemon. Brush both sides of the trout with mustard mixture. Coat the fish on both sides with the

Feast #15

seasoned bread crumbs and press firmly to adhere the crumbs to the fish.

— Coat a large skillet with ¼ to ½ inch of olive oil and bring to a medium-high heat. Add the fish to the pan, two at a time, skin side down, and cook the fish two-thirds of the way, about 6 to 7 minutes. Carefully turn the fish over and cook the other side until the fish is brown and crispy, about 2 to 3 minutes. Remove the fish from the pan and drain on paper towels. After the first batch is done and drained on paper towels, reserve it on a rack in a warm oven.

— When all the fish has been fried, remove the oil and any brown bits from the pan. Add the butter and remaining lemon juice and swirl to combine as the butter melts. Season with salt to taste, and reduce by about half. Transfer the fish to a serving platter. Drizzle with the butter lemon sauce and serve.

Mignonette Sauce
(serve in a small side bowl)
* I tablespoon coarsely ground black pepper
* ½ cup red wine vinegar
* 2 tablespoons finely minced shallots
* Sea salt to taste

— Mix in a small bowl, cover, and refrigerate until serving time.

RUTABAGA MASH

Makes 8 servings

A cross between a cabbage and a turnip, this large, solid root vegetable makes a great mash with more character than a potato. POW!

* I ½ pounds rutabagas, peeled, cut into ½-inch pieces
* 2 large carrots, peeled, thinly sliced
* I large garlic clove, peeled
* I bay leaf
* 3 tablespoons butter
* 2 tablespoons chopped fresh parsley

— Boil rutabagas and carrots with garlic and bay leaf in a large pan of barely salted water until tender. Remove and discard the bay leaf. Drain, then add butter and mash with a potato masher or a stick blender. Top with parsley and serve.

BRAISED RAMPS

This spring vegetable is sometimes called a wild leek, but whatever you call them, when you see them in the farmer's market, or in the field, buy them. They have a delicate onion aroma and flavor. We love them.

* I cup grape-seed oil
* 2 pounds ramps (approximately 6 bunches), cleaned and drained
* Salt and freshly ground black pepper to taste

— Place oil in a large, shallow pan with a tight-fitting lid over high heat. When oil is warm, roll a bunch of ramps in paper towels to remove excess moisture, and unwrap. Reduce heat to medium, and add ramps to pan. Toss to coat each leaf with oil. Working quickly, dry second bunch and add to the oil, tossing until ramps wilt. Continue with remaining ramps, adding more oil as needed.

- When all ramps are wilted, season to taste and reduce heat to low, then stir and cover pot. Cook 5 to 10 minutes, depending on the size of the ramps, stirring frequently to avoid burning. When ramps are very, very tender, remove pan from heat and let sit, covered, for 10 minutes. Season again if desired, and serve.

MANGO SORBET

Get out the ice-cream maker and get ready for warm weather desserts.

* 4 cups ripe mangos, peeled and chopped (makes 3-½ cups)
* I cup simple syrup*
* Juice and grated zest of 4 limes

- Combine mangos, syrup, lime juice, and zest in an electric ice-cream maker and process until the sorbet is frozen. Store in the freezer until serving time.

- *To make simple syrup, stir together 2 cups granulated sugar and 2 cups water in a small saucepan, cook and stir until thoroughly combined. Cool and store in a jar in the refrigerator up to a week.

Smothered Spring Vegetables with Turkey Wings

✳ Braised Turkey Wings with Smothered Red Cabbage and Escarole

✳ Roasted Spring Roots, including radishes, broccoli, peppers, and fennel

✳ Rhubarb Strawberry Cobbler

BRAISED TURKEY WINGS WITH SMOTHERED RED CABBAGE AND ESCAROLE

Makes 8 servings

Golden brown wings on top of a bed of aromatic cabbage and escarole will buckle your knees before you take the first bite. Yes.

* 2 tablespoons grape-seed oil
* 2-3 smoked turkey wings (cut into thirds at the joint)
* sea salt and freshly ground black pepper to taste
* 2 cups finely chopped yellow onion and carrot (peeled and finely sliced into matchsticks)
* 2 teaspoons toasted cumin seeds
* 8 cups red cabbage (sliced ¼-inch thick)
* I large head escarole, chopped
* 2 cups tart apples (grated on the large holes of a box grater)
* ¼ cup red wine vinegar
* I cup freshly squeezed orange juice
* ¼ cup brown sugar
* 2 tablespoons Dijon mustard

– Preheat 325°F.

– Place a Dutch oven over medium-high heat. When the pan is hot, add the olive oil along with the smoked turkey wings. Cook until the wings are golden brown on each side, then remove from the pot and set aside. Add the onions and carrots and a pinch of salt. Push them to one side of the pan and add the cumin seeds to the pan to toast for 2 minutes. Stir together and cook until the vegetables begin to soften (5 minutes). Stir in the cabbage, escarole, and apples. Add the turkey wings back into the pot. Cover and cook until the cabbage starts to wilt (3-5 minutes).

— In the meantime, whisk together the orange juice and brown sugar. Reduce the heat to medium low. Pour into the cabbage mixture and season with a good amount of salt and pepper. Add the vinegar to the pot. Cover the pot and place in the oven to cook for 45 minutes. Stir in the mustard, then taste for seasoning, adding more salt and pepper if necessary. Serve the cabbage with the smoked turkey wings on top.

ROASTED SPRING ROOTS, INCLUDING RADISHES, BROCCOLI, PEPPERS, AND FENNEL

Makes 8 servings

* I bunch radishes, tops removed and reserved
* I head broccoli and cauliflower, chopped, including stems
* I large fennel bulb, sliced fine
* 2 small red peppers, chopped
* 2 tablespoons honey
* 2 tablespoons unsalted butter, melted
* I tablespoon apple cider vinegar
* sea salt and freshly ground black pepper to taste
* ¼ cup fresh thyme, chopped

— Position a rack in the center of the oven and set a 12-inch ovenproof skillet (preferably cast iron) on the rack. Heat the oven to 450°F.

— Trim the radishes and then halve or quarter them lengthwise, depending on their size. Trim and discard the stems from the tops, wash the leaves thoroughly, and pat dry or dry in a salad spinner. Repeat with broccoli, cauliflower, fennel, and red peppers.

— In a medium bowl, combine the honey, butter, vinegar, and ½ teaspoon salt and pepper. Add thyme, and then add the radishes and other vegetables and toss until coated. Transfer to the hot skillet, spread in a single layer, and roast in the hot oven, stirring occasionally, until the vegetables are crisp-tender, 15 to 20 minutes. Remove from the oven. Add the radish tops and thyme leaves, and toss until the leaves are just wilted; serve.

RHUBARB STRAWBERRY COBBLER

Makes 8 servings

Nothing says spring like a dessert made from rhubarb and strawberries.

* 2 pints strawberries, hulled and thickly sliced
* 8 ounces rhubarb, trimmed and cut into ½-inch pieces (2 cups)
* ½ cup granulated sugar
* 2 tablespoons quick-cooking tapioca, or I tablespoon cornstarch
* ⅛ teaspoon EACH: ground cinnamon, nutmeg, ginger

Topping

* 1½ cups all-purpose flour
* ¼ cup plus 1 tablespoon granulated sugar, divided
* 1½ teaspoons baking powder
* ½ teaspoon baking soda and salt
* ¼ teaspoon EACH: ground cinnamon, ginger, and nutmeg
* 2 tablespoons cold butter, cut into pieces
* 1 cup nonfat buttermilk

- To prepare filling: Combine strawberries, rhubarb, ½ cup granulated sugar, tapioca (or cornstarch), ⅛ teaspoon cinnamon, ⅛ teaspoon ginger, and ⅛ teaspoon nutmeg in a 9-inch deep-dish pie pan and let stand for 20 minutes.

- Preheat oven to 400°F.

- To prepare topping: Stir together flour, ¼ cup granulated sugar, baking powder, baking soda, salt, ¼ teaspoon cinnamon, ¼ teaspoon ginger and nutmeg in a large bowl. Cut butter into dry ingredients with a pastry cutter, 2 forks, or your fingers until crumbly. Use a fork to stir in buttermilk just until combined.

- Using a large spoon, drop the dough in 8 dollops over the filling. Sprinkle with the remaining 1 tablespoon granulated sugar. Bake the cobbler on the middle rack of the hot oven until browned and bubbling, 40 to 50 minutes. (Cover with foil if the top is browning too quickly.) Cool slightly on a wire rack. Serve warm.

Tristan's Birthday Faves

The artist in our family is Tristan, who could draw before he could walk, and sing before he could talk. He is our firstborn son and our treasure. We pull out all the stops to celebrate his birthday. He always asks for my fried chicken with waffles.

* Southern Fried Chicken with Sweet Potato Waffles
* Tri-Color Cole Slaw
* Tristan's Special Peach Cobbler

When I was growing up, my mama and my aunt Ella Mae both made great fried chicken; so did my aunt Minnie Mae, and don't forget Aunt Mary. They fried the best chicken and each had her own version. But after tasting a lot of chicken all around, I learned to use the methods I learned working in French kitchens. This means I brine my chicken overnight, then rinse, drain, and leave it in a buttermilk soak for the day. I'd have to say that this is a perfect example of what happens when the French chef shakes hands with his Southern cousins.

My method takes two days, but only about 20 minutes of your time, and the result is mouthwatering, with a deep, layered flavor and cooked through. The actual chicken frying is done in 10 to 15 minutes, but the preparation is mostly a matter of brining and soaking. Easy and well worth the extra steps.

The first time I fried chicken my way for Tristan's birthday, he was surprised. POW! I told him. Now that's giving it my little twist.

When it comes time to fry a chicken, I choose a smaller bird, or chicken pieces, so that the pieces will cook evenly. After brining and soaking, I just give it a quick pass through my Chef Jesse dredge and then fry that baby up. Ready to eat in 10 to 15 minutes.

Feast #17

I always use a deep fat thermometer in the oil, and an instant-read thermometer to stick in the bird to make sure it's cooked through. Tiny steps, but the result is worth it. It's important not to overload the skillet because that drops the oil temperature and results in a greasy bird. Using a 10-inch deep, heavy black skillet, preheat the oil, then fry four pieces at a time. Then drain and fry the other four.

POW! Serve that baby with some sweet potato waffles and coleslaw. Now you're talking.

SOUTHERN FRIED CHICKEN

* 3- to 4-pound frying chicken cut into 8 pieces (or use pieces — say, legs and thighs, breasts, around 3-4 pounds)
* I quart buttermilk
* I teaspoon hot sauce (Frank's is good)

Chef Jesse's Fried Chicken Spice Blend
To make the blend

* 2 teaspoons EACH: paprika, granulated garlic, and granulated onion
* I teaspoon EACH: black and white pepper + fresh thyme
* 2 cups all-purpose flour
* 2 tablespoons cornstarch

– Prepare the dredge by blending the dried herbs with the flour and cornstarch in a shallow bowl or brown paper or plastic bag.

– The day before you plan to serve, fill a large bowl with cold water and add ¼

cup kosher salt. Put chicken pieces in the brine and refrigerate, The next morning, lift the chicken out of the brine. Rinse and drain. Now place brined chicken in a bowl and cover with buttermilk. Add hot sauce. Soak in the refrigerator about 8 hours. Then drain.

– Place chicken pieces in the dredge, shake well to coat the pieces, and shake off excess flour.

– In a 5-quart heavy pot or deep skillet, add 48 ounces peanut, soy, or other vegetable oil and heat over medium-high heat to 365°F. Cook four pieces at a time, turning once, until golden brown and cooked through to an internal temperature of 140°F.

– Fry for 10 to 15 minutes, turning, then drain on paper towels or a wire rack. POW! Serve with additional hot sauce.

CHEF JESSE'S SWEET POTATO WAFFLES

* 2 cups cake flour
* 3 teaspoons baking powder
* ½ teaspoon salt
* I teaspoon cinnamon
* ½ teaspoon allspice
* I tablespoon granulated sugar
* 2 teaspoons light brown sugar
* 3 large egg yolks, separated, save whites
* I½ cups buttermilk
* ½ cup unsalted butter, melted
* ½ cup vegetable oil
* ½ teaspoon pure vanilla extract
* I small sweet potato, baked, peeled, and mashed (about 4 ounces)

- Preheat the waffle iron.

- Sift together flour, baking powder, salt, cinnamon, and allspice and pour into a bowl.

- In a second bowl combine egg yolks, buttermilk, melted butter, oil, vanilla, and sweet potato.

- Add liquid ingredients to dry ingredients and mix gently until combined. Don't overmix. Beat the egg whites until frothy and fluffy and gently fold into waffle mix. Let rest a few minutes.

- Spray the waffle iron with oil and ladle 4 to 6 ounces of batter. Add more batter until it fills the spaces. Close and cook until golden.

- Serve waffles with fried chicken on top. POW!

TRI-COLOR COLE SLAW

You eat with your eyes first, and once you see this brightly colored slaw, you'll never want to go back to plain old cabbage.

* I carrot, peeled and grated
* ½ head green cabbage (about I pound), quartered, cored, and thinly sliced
* ½ head red cabbage (about I pound), quartered, cored, and thinly sliced
* I small red onion, peeled and very thinly sliced
* ½ cup chopped parsley
* 2 teaspoons kosher salt
* ¼ cup extra-virgin olive oil
* 2 tablespoons red wine vinegar
* I tablespoon celery seed
* I tablespoon granulated sugar

- In a large colander, toss together carrot, cabbage, onion, parsley, and salt. Set colander over a large bowl and let sit 30 minutes; press firmly to remove moisture.

- In a large bowl, whisk together oil, vinegar, celery seed, and granulated sugar to combine, then add cabbage mixture and toss well to coat. Cover and chill at least 2 hours, then serve.

TRISTAN'S PEACH COBBLER

When the peaches come in, there is nothing better than homemade peach cobbler. You can tell the peaches are ripe when you can smell them in the farmer's market from a good distance. POW!

Makes 8 servings

* I cup granulated sugar
* ¼ cup brown sugar
* ½ cup all-purpose flour + more to sprinkle
* ¼ teaspoon ground nutmeg
* ⅛ teaspoon ground cloves
* I teaspoon ground cinnamon
* ½ cup unsalted butter (I stick)
* I ½ cup peach juice
* 5 cups fresh peaches, peeled, pitted, and sliced
* I teaspoon pure vanilla extract
* I teaspoon fresh lemon juice + grated zest of ½ lemon

- To make filling, combine white and brown sugars, with flour, nutmeg, cloves and cinnamon in a bowl.

- Melt butter in a large Dutch oven. Add sugar mixture, peach juice and peaches. Stir to combine. Simmer over low heat until the peaches are tender, about 10 minutes. Add vanilla, lemon juice and grated lemon zest. Set it aside.

- Preheat the oven to 375° F.

To make the biscuit dough:

* 2-1/4 cups all-purpose flour
* 2 teaspoons baking powder
* ½ teaspoon sea salt
* 1 cup cold butter (2 sticks), cut into small chunks
* ½ cup (may need a few drops more) ice water

- To make the biscuit dough, add flour, baking powder and salt to a large bowl or a food processor. Process (or rub dough between your fingers) until it resembles coarse meal. (no more than 10-12 pulses) Sprinkle with ice water and stir to barely combine. (Do not overwork the dough or it will be tough.)

- Cover with plastic wrap and let it sit for 30 minutes or so.

- Then divide the dough. Roll out half onto a barely floured board. Transfer the dough to the bottom of the 9 x 13 pan and roll out to be ¼-inch thick. Using a fork, pierce a few holes into the bottom layer and bake for 12 minutes. Remove from the oven and pour in peach filing. Roll the second dough, and add on top, piercing a few holes with a fork, bake until golden brown about 25 to 30 minutes.

(Here's a tip... Once you have rolled out the dough, roll it onto the rolling pin to transfer to the baking pan. Then once you have the peach filling inside, roll the second sheet of dough and roll it onto the pin to easily transfer to the to of the pan.)

- Serve warm with ice cream or whipped cream.

Chapter 6: June

June Is Busting Out All Over

Juneteenth *has been celebrated for more than 150 years as a day of freedom for African-Americans. That party started in 1865, more than two years after Abraham Lincoln issued the Emancipation Proclamation. It took nearly two years for word to get to Galveston, but those Texans always knew how to throw a party, and so declared June 19th as a day for rest and relaxation. Still in Texas, they throw parades, barbecues, and backyard parties. But the celebration of Juneteenth has spread across the South and all over the country. Let's hear it for freedom and equality for all.*

Break Out the Grill

First time using the grill for the season? How about a Trinidadian special—jerk chicken. So what the heck is jerk chicken, you ask? That's easy. It comes from those tropical islands where preserving food was hard before refrigeration. So what to do? Often they rubbed chickens and other meats in a spicy mixture that not only flavored the food, but preserved it as well.

* Grilled Jerk Chicken

* Fresh Mango Salad

* Caribbean Rice and Beans

* Fried Plantains with a Brown Sugar Glaze

* Lemon Berry Savarin

GRILLED JERK CHICKEN

Makes 8 servings

* 6 to 8 chicken breasts, thighs, or legs

– Rub the chicken with the jerk spice and marinate in the refrigerator overnight.

To make the jerk spice blend (yields about ½ cup)

* ½ teaspoon coriander seeds
* 5 whole cloves
* 6 cardamom pods
* 10 allspice berries
* ½ teaspoon black pepper
* 2 bay leaves, crumbled
* ½ stick cinnamon, crushed into small pieces

* 4 cloves garlic
* 8 jalapeño peppers, toasted and seeded (or to taste)
* I inch fresh ginger, peeled
* ½ tablespoon fresh thyme

— Toast dry spices on a small tray in the oven at 350°F, for about 10 minutes, or until aromas are released. Puree spices with garlic, jalapeños, ginger, and thyme. Add small amount of water to make a paste.

— Cook the marinated chicken on a hot grill for 10 minutes, turn the chicken over, and cook for 10 minutes more, or until completely done. Keep hot.

FRESH MANGO SALSA

Makes 6-8 servings

* 3 teaspoons white balsamic vinegar
* 3 teaspoons fresh lemon juice
* 2 teaspoons granulated sugar
* ½ teaspoon kosher salt
* ½ teaspoon freshly ground black pepper
* 4 tablespoons extra-virgin olive oil
* 3 (I pound) firm-ripe mangoes, peeled and cut into ½-inch pieces
* 2 large tomatoes, cut into ½-inch pieces
* 2 small red onions, halved lengthwise and thinly sliced crosswise
* ⅔ cup fresh cilantro leaves

— Whisk together vinegar, lemon juice, granulated sugar, salt, and pepper until sugar is dissolved, then add oil, whisking until emulsified. Add remaining ingredients and toss until coated.

CARIBBEAN RICE AND BEANS

Makes 6 servings

The authentic Caribbean method in the Islands is to start off with pigeon peas, but you can use whatever you like.

* 2 cups dried beans of your choice (white, black, pinto, cannellini)
* 2 tablespoons grape-seed oil
* I small onion, chopped
* 3 cloves garlic, minced
* I cup long grain white rice
* 2 cups chicken stock
* I 15-ounce can coconut milk
* I teaspoon ground cumin
* ½ teaspoon chopped cilantro, or to taste

— Soak beans overnight in water to cover. Drain beans and transfer to a medium pot. Cover with water and boil until tender, about 2 hours.

— Heat oil in a saucepan over medium heat. Cook and stir onion and garlic in hot oil until softened, 5 to 7 minutes. Add rice. Cook and stir a few minutes, or until rice begins to turn golden.

— Stir broth, coconut milk, beans, and cumin into the rice, onion, and garlic mixture. Bring to a boil. Cover and simmer until the rice is tender and the moisture is absorbed, about 20 minutes.

— Gently stir cilantro into the beans and rice.

FRIED PLANTAINS WITH BROWN SUGAR GLAZE

Makes 6 to 8 servings

* 2-3 plantains, really ripe with black marks
* olive oil
* 2 tablespoons butter
* 2 tablespoons brown sugar
* 1 ounce rum
* Dash sea salt
* Splash lime juice

– Peel and slice the plantain in half and then long ways. Fill a saucepan with about a half inch of oil. Fry the plantains on each side for just a few seconds, until brown. Drain on paper towels.

– For the glaze, melt the butter with the brown sugar and whisk until it dissolves. Add the rum and allow to boil until most of the alcohol cooks out, about 2 minutes. Swirl the pot or whisk the mixture so that it does not burn. Season with a sprinkling of sea salt and a splash of lime juice.

– Drizzle over the plantains and enjoy.

LEMON BERRY SAVARIN

Makes 6 to 8 servings

Bread
* 1 tablespoon active dry yeast
* ¼ cup warm water
* 1½ cups unbleached all-purpose flour
* 3 tablespoons granulated sugar
* ½ teaspoon sea salt
* 3 large eggs, room temperature
* ½ cup (8 tablespoons) unsalted butter, soft

Syrup
* 1 cup boiling water
* ¾ cup granulated sugar
* 2 tablespoons lemon juice
* ¼ cup kirsch or another cherry-flavored liqueur

Topping
* ¼ cup red currant jelly
* 4 cups (2 pints) strawberries
* whipped cream, crème fraiche, or fresh yogurt

To make the bread:

– In a large bowl, stir the yeast into warm water to soften.

– Add the flour, granulated sugar, salt, and eggs to the yeast mixture. Beat for 2 minutes.

– Cut the butter into eight pieces. Add one piece at a time to the yeast mixture. Beat well after each addition. Cover with plastic wrap and refrigerate for 2 hours.

– Press the dough down and scrape into a well-greased 6-cup savarin mold or Bundt pan. Cover and let rise for 1½ hours.

– While the savarin is rising, preheat the oven to 375°F.

– Bake for 35 minutes, or until it is golden and firm to the touch.

– Remove the savarin from the mold and let it cool on a rack.

– While it's cooling, make the syrup. Combine the boiling water, granulated sugar, and lemon juice. Stir until the sugar dissolves.

- Bring the mixture to a rolling boil over high heat. Reduce heat to medium and cook for 5 minutes.

- Remove from heat. Add the kirsch.

- Pour ½ cup of syrup into the savarin mold. Put the savarin back in the mold. Spoon the syrup over the top until the savarin has absorbed all the syrup. Let sit for 20 minutes.

- Remove the savarin from the mold.

- Heat the jelly to a liquid state. Brush on all sides of the savarin.

- Serve with fresh strawberries and large dollops of whipped cream, crème fraîche, or yogurt.

Burgers with a Bite

＊ Spicy Lamb Burger Sliders with Harissa

＊ Sweet Potato Fries

＊ Tomato Cucumber Salad with Mint Apple Cider Vinaigrette

＊ Lemon Squares

SPICY LAMB BURGER SLIDERS WITH HARISSA

Makes 4 to 6 servings

You can make little bite-sized sliders or regular-sized burgers. Your choice.

* 2 pounds ground lamb
* 4 tablespoons grated yellow onion, with juice
* I clove garlic, finely chopped
* I tablespoon EACH: sweet smoked paprika, ground cumin, coriander, and harissa
* I teaspoon cinnamon
* Sea salt and freshly ground black pepper to taste
* 6 to 8 sharp cheddar slices
* 8 to 12 small hamburger rolls
* Red onion slices
* Thin sliced tomatoes
* Parsley

— In a large bowl, combine the lamb, onion, garlic, paprika, cumin, coriander, harissa, cinnamon, and salt and pepper. Divide into 6 to 8 equal portions, then form each portion into a patty. Drizzle with olive oil.

— Heat a large cast-iron skillet or grill pan over medium- high heat. Add the patties and cook, turning once, for 4 minutes for medium. Toast roll tops on the grill as well. During the last minute of cooking, divide the cheese among the patties and tent with foil to melt. Top the rolls with the patties, red onion, tomatoes, and parsley. Then add tops and serve at once.

SWEET POTATO FRIES

Makes 6 servings

* 4 large sweet potatoes, scrubbed clean
* 2 tablespoons grape-seed oil
* ½ teaspoon sea salt
* 1½ teaspoon EACH: garlic powder, smoked paprika, and dried oregano
* 1 teaspoon dried (or 2 teaspoons fresh) thyme
* ¼ teaspoon EACH black pepper and cayenne pepper

- Preheat oven to 425 degrees F.

- Leave the skin on and cut sweet potatoes with a sharp knife into thin, even matchsticks.

- Transfer to two baking sheets and drizzle with grape-seed oil. Then sprinkle with seasonings, and toss. Arrange in a single layer to ensure they crisp up.

- Bake for 15 minutes and flip/stir to cook on the other side. Bake for 10 to 15 minutes more, or until brown and crispy. You'll know they're done when the edges are dark brown and crispy.

- Remove from oven.

- Serve plain or with your favorite ketchup.

MARINATED TOMATO CUCUMBER SALAD WITH MINT APPLE CIDER VINAIGRETTE

Makes 6 servings

* 3 English (also known as hothouse) cucumbers, peeled and sliced
* ⅓ cup red onion, peeled and very thinly sliced (optional)
* 1 cup water
* ½ cup apple cider vinegar
* 2 tablespoons granulated sugar
* 2 teaspoons sea salt
* 1 teaspoon freshly milled black pepper
* ¼ cup grape-seed oil
* 3 medium tomatoes, chopped (or 2-3 cups of any tomato you like)
* ¼ cup chopped fresh mint

- Place the cucumbers and red onion in a bowl. Whisk together the water, vinegar, granulated sugar, salt, pepper, and oil until the sugar is dissolved. Pour over the cucumbers and onions and let sit in the refrigerator for at least 30 minutes or up to 3 hours.

- Pour off all but a few tablespoons of the liquid. Add the tomatoes and herbs and toss to combine. Serve and enjoy!

LEMON SQUARES

Makes 24 small squares

Crust
* Grape-seed oil, for greasing
* 1½ sticks unsalted butter, diced
* 2 cups all-purpose flour

* ¼ cup packed light brown sugar
* ½ cup confectioner's sugar, plus more for garnish
* ¼ teaspoon sea salt

Filling:
* 4 large eggs, plus 2 egg yolks
* 2 cups granulated sugar
* ⅓ cup all-purpose flour, sifted
* 1 teaspoon grated lemon zest
* 1 cup fresh lemon juice (from about 8 lemons)

- Make the crust: Position a rack in the middle of the oven and preheat to 350 degrees F. Grease a 9 x 13 pan with oil and line with foil, leaving a 2-inch overhang on all sides; grease the foil with oil. Pulse the butter, flour, both sugars, and the salt in a food processor until the dough comes together, about 1 minute. Press evenly into the bottom and about ½ inch up the sides of the prepared pan, making sure there are no cracks. Bake until the crust is golden, about 25 minutes.

- Meanwhile, make the filling: Whisk the whole eggs and yolks, granulated sugar, and flour in a bowl until smooth. Whisk in the lemon zest and juice. Remove the crust from the oven and reduce the temperature to 300 degrees F. Pour the filling over the warm crust and return to the oven. Bake until the filling is just set, 30 to 35 minutes.

- Let the bars cool in the pan on a rack, then refrigerate until firm, at least 2 hours. Lift out of the pan using the foil and slice. Dust with confectioners' sugar before serving.

Chapter 7: July

Fourth of July Cold Lunch

* Easy Pickled Shrimp
* Iceberg Wedge Bits with Blue Cheese
* Corn Bread (SEE PAGE 70 FOR RECIPE)
* Favorite Bananas Foster

EASY PICKLED SHRIMP

You can make this up to a day ahead, but you'll have to keep your hungry helpers out of it. So tempting.

Makes 8 servings

* 2 pounds raw shrimp, medium

Pickling mixture:
* I cup unseasoned rice vinegar
* I cup olive oil
* ¼ cup EACH: fresh lemon juice, paper-thin lemon slices, red onion slices, and peeled garlic cloves (about I large head)
* 3 fresh bay leaves, coarsely torn
* 3 teaspoons EACH: celery seeds and mustard seeds
* I teaspoon coarse kosher salt
* ½ teaspoon freshly ground black pepper

Boiling mixture:

* 8 cups water
* I cup coarse kosher salt
* 10 bay leaves
* 6 fresh thyme sprigs
* I unpeeled whole head of garlic, cut crosswise in half
* ¼ cup paprika
* 2 tablespoons mustard seeds
* I tablespoon EACH: whole allspice, celery seeds, and cardamom pods
* I cinnamon stick
* 2 pounds uncooked medium OR large shrimp in shells
* Ice cubes
* Crusty bread

For pickling mixture:

– Stir rice vinegar, olive oil, lemon juice, lemon slices, onion slices, garlic cloves, bay leaves, celery seeds, mustard seeds, coarse kosher salt, and black pepper in large bowl until salt dissolves. Chill.

– DO AHEAD: *Can be made 1 day ahead.* Cover and refrigerate overnight.

For boiling mixture:

– Place 8 cups water in large pot. Add coarse salt, bay leaves, thyme sprigs, garlic, paprika, mustard seeds, allspice, celery seeds, cardamom pods, and cinnamon stick. Bring to boil over high heat. Boil 5 minutes. Add shrimp; stir to separate. Boil just until shells turn pink, about 2 minutes. Using large skimmer, transfer shrimp to colander to drain.

– Line rimmed baking sheet with layer of ice cubes. Scatter shrimp on ice to cool quickly, about 5 minutes. Peel and devein shrimp, leaving tails intact. Add peeled shrimp to pickling mixture. Stir to blend. Cover and refrigerate at least 3 hours and up to 6 hours.

– Using slotted spoon, lift shrimp from pickling mixture. Arrange on platter. Serve with crusty bread.

ICEBERG WEDGE BITES WITH BLUE CHEESE AND CORN BREAD

Makes 8 servings

* I large head iceberg lettuce, cut into 8 wedges

Blue Cheese Dressing

* ⅔ cup buttermilk, well shaken
* ⅓ cup mayonnaise
* 4 ounces crumbled blue cheese (about I cup)
* I tablespoon lemon juice
* A few dashes hot sauce, such as Tabasco
* 2 tablespoons chopped chives
* Sea salt and freshly milled black pepper, to taste

– In a bowl, combine buttermilk, mayonnaise, half of the blue cheese, lemon juice, and hot sauce.

– Stir to combine and add chives, salt and pepper.

– Then drizzle over iceberg wedges and top with remaining blue cheese.

FAVORITE BANANAS FOSTER

Makes 8 servings

So easy and so satisfying.

* ¼ cup (½ stick) butter
* I cup brown sugar
* ½ teaspoon cinnamon
* ¼ cup banana liqueur (good brand)
* 8 bananas cut in half lengthwise, then halved
* ½ cup dark Myers' Rum

— Serve over vanilla ice cream

— Combine the butter, brown sugar, and cinnamon in a flambé pan or skillet. Place the pan over low heat on top of the stove and cook, stirring until sugar dissolves. Stir in banana liqueur; then place the bananas in the pan. When the banana sections soften and begin to brown, carefully add the rum.

— Continue to cook the sauce until the rum is hot; then tip the pan slightly to ignite the rum. When the flames subside, lift the bananas out of the pan and place four pieces over each portion of ice cream. Generously spoon warm sauce over the top of the ice cream and serve.

Grilling in the Garden

✳ Grilled Flank Steak

✳ Arugula and Beefsteak Tomato Salad

✳ Grilled Peaches with Bourbon Butter Sauce and Vanilla Ice Cream

GRILLED FLANK STEAK

Makes 6 servings

* ✳ I cup port wine
* ✳ ½ cup EACH: chopped shallots and grape-seed oil
* ✳ 2 tablespoons EACH: fresh parsley, oregano, and thyme
* ✳ I bay leaf
* ✳ 4 cloves garlic, minced
* ✳ I teaspoon EACH: white, black, and cayenne pepper
* ✳ ½ teaspoon Creole mustard
* ✳ I 2- to 4-pound flank steak, trimmed and fat discarded

— Mix all ingredients except steak in 13 x 9 x 2 glass baking dish. Add steak and turn to coat. Cover and refrigerate 2 hours or overnight, turning occasionally.

— Prepare barbeque (medium-high heat) or preheat the broiler. Remove meat from marinade; discard marinade. Grill the steak to desired doneness, about 4 minutes per side for medium rare. (OR oven bake about 12 minutes at 375°F.)

— Transfer steak to work surface. Let it rest about 5 minutes. Cut across the grain into thin strips. Arrange on platter and serve.

ARUGULA AND BEEFSTEAK TOMATO SALAD

* 2 pounds beefsteak tomatoes
* 3 tablespoons EACH: red wine vinegar and extra-virgin olive oil
* Coarse sea salt and freshly ground black pepper
* 1 bunch arugula (6 to 8 ounces), washed well and dried

- Core beefsteak tomatoes; cut each into 8 wedges.

- In a small bowl, whisk together vinegar and oil; season with salt and pepper. In a large bowl, toss arugula with half the dressing. Divide arugula and tomatoes evenly among four serving plates or a serving platter. Drizzle tomatoes with remaining dressing. Serve immediately.

GRILLED PEACHES WITH BOURBON BUTTER SAUCE AND VANILLA ICE CREAM

So easy to do, it will buckle your knees.

Makes 6 to 8 servings

* 3-4 ripe peaches (optionally peeled)
* 3 tablespoons butter
* ¾ cup brown sugar
* ¾ cup bourbon
* 1 tsp cinnamon
* pinch of salt
* Optional Topping – whipped cream or vanilla ice cream

- Peel the peaches if you'd like, then cut each in half and remove the pit. Put peaches aside on a dish to await grilling.

- Combine butter, brown sugar, bourbon, and cinnamon in a medium saucepan on the stovetop over medium heat. Heat and stir until the sugar is completely dissolved and the sauce is hot and bubbly. Pour into a small pitcher to await serving.

- Grill peaches on a hot oiled grill for approximately 3-4 minutes. Remove from the grill and serve with warm bourbon butter sauce and whipped cream or ice cream.

Roast it Right Up

* Roast Chicken with Herbes de Provence
* Red Potatoes with Parsley
* Green Beans with Hazelnuts
* Homemade Silky Strawberry Sorbet

ROAST CHICKEN WITH HERBES DE PROVENCE

Makes 6 to 8 servings with plenty of leftovers for chicken soup or salad

* I roasting chicken, 4 to 6 pounds
* 3 garlic cloves, smashed
* I teaspoon EACH: sea salt and freshly cracked black pepper
* I teaspoon herbes de provence*
* Soft butter to rub the skin

— Heat the oven to 350°F.

— Wash and dry the chicken. Place in a large roaster on its back.

— Peel the garlic cloves by whacking with the flat of a knife. Put the garlic into the chicken's cavity, then sprinkle with salt and pepper. Add the herbes de provence. Spread soft butter over the chicken breast.

— Roast, covered, at 350°F for 60-90 minutes depending on the size of the chicken. Remove the lid and roast uncovered another 15-30 minutes until the skin is crisp and the chicken is fully cooked. Use an instant-read thermometer to check the temperature. Cook to 150°F at the thickest part of the thigh. Remove from the oven and let it rest on a cutting board up to 30 minutes before carving.

— Make au jus by dissolving a tablespoon of cornstarch in a little water. Stir that into the pan juices and raise to a boil. Taste and adjust seasonings with salt and pepper. Transfer the sauce to a gravy boat for serving.

* Herbes de provence are a dry mixture of savory herbs including savory, thyme, rosemary, and bay leaves. It is often sold in good grocery stores in little cloth bags. To use, just drop this into the cavity of the bird. Want to make your own? Just make your own mixture of the dry herbs, and rub the cavity of the bird with this classic French seasoning.

RED POTATOES WITH PARSLEY

Almost too easy to be called a recipe. Simply buy one red potato for each diner plus a couple for the pot. Scrub potatoes, then steam until tender, about 15-20 minutes.

Meanwhile mince a tablespoon or so of fresh parsley. Transfer potatoes to a serving bowl and top with parsley, melted butter, and black pepper. POW!

GREEN BEANS WITH HAZELNUTS

Another side dish that's so easy it is barely a recipe. Pick up a couple of handfuls of fresh green beans at the farmer's market.

Steam until just tender, no more than 2-3 minutes, then blanch in an ice water bath to stop the cooking.

Transfer to a serving bowl. Top with chopped hazelnuts and salt and pepper to taste. Easy, huh?

HOMEMADE SILKY STRAWBERRY SORBET

No need for an ice-cream maker here. Just whiz up the berries using a stick blender, heat with cornstarch mixture, then freeze the mixture in a flat dish for a couple of hours or overnight. Then whiz it up again with a stick blender. POW! Pure silk and just as delicious as it is beautiful. Serve in ice cream bowls.

Makes 6 to 8 servings

* 1 large basket of strawberries, hulled and quartered
* ½ cup granulated sugar or to taste
* 1 pinch salt
* 1½ teaspoons cornstarch
* 1½ teaspoons cold water
* 3 tablespoons lemon juice

– Place berries in a work bowl and puree until smooth using a stick blender. Combine berry puree, granulated sugar, and salt in a large saucepan. Heat until melted and just simmering. Whisk cornstarch into the cold water; stir into heated berry mixture. Remove from heat, and stir in lemon juice. Cool slightly. Freeze berry mixture until cold and slushy, about 2 hours.

– To serve, make a silky cold mixture using the stick blender. Serve immediately.

Summer Sandwiches

* Chef Jesse's Crockpot-Style North Carolina Pulled Pork on Mini-Brioche Rolls
* Creole Green Beans (SEE PAGE 78 FOR RECIPE)
* Old-Fashioned Hummingbird Layer Cake

CHEF JESSE'S CROCKPOT-STYLE NORTH CAROLINA PULLED PORK ON MINI-BRIOCHE ROLLS

Makes 8 servings

* 2 tablespoons brown sugar
* 1 teaspoon smoked paprika
* 2 teaspoons kosher salt
* 1 teaspoon EACH: granulated garlic and onion
* ½ teaspoon EACH: ground black pepper and crushed red pepper
* 1 4- to 6-pound pork butt or shoulder roast
* 2 large yellow onions, quartered
* 1 cup EACH: cider vinegar, ketchup, and chili sauce
* ½ cup creole mustard
* ⅓ cup Worcestershire sauce

– Blend brown sugar, paprika, salt, garlic, onion, black pepper, crushed pepper, and rub over the roast. Cover with plastic wrap in a shallow glass pan, and marinate overnight in the refrigerator.

Next day:

– Place onions in Crockpot, then add marinated roast.

– Combine vinegar, ketchup, chili sauce, creole mustard, and Worcestershire sauce. Stir to mix well. Pour about ½ of mixture over roast. Save the rest for later.

– Cover the pot. Cook the roast on low for 8-10 hours. Remove meat and onions, discard the onions, and shred the meat. Add juices from Crockpot

Feast #23

and some remaining vinegar mixture to moisten the meat. Save some to pass at the table. Serve on mini-brioche rolls.

OLD-FASHIONED HUMMINGBIRD LAYER CAKEE

Makes a large three-layer cake to serve 12 to 16

A true child of the South recipe, the banana, coconut, and pineapple flavors in this cake came up from the tropics and took over the hearts of Southern bakers about the time my grandmother learned to bake. I have always loved it.

This is one way to use up those black overripe bananas.

* Nonstick baking spray
* 2 sticks (I cup) butter, softened
* 2 cups granulated sugar
* I tablespoon vanilla extract
* 4 large eggs
* 3 cups all-purpose flour
* I teaspoon baking soda
* I teaspoon ground cinnamon
* I teaspoon salt
* ⅓ cup buttermilk
* 1½ cups mashed overripe bananas (about 4 medium)
* I 8-ounce can crushed pineapple and juice
* Optional garnishes: sweetened flaked coconut, pecans

Frosting:
* 2 sticks (I cup) butter, softened
* 2 8-ounce packages cream cheese, softened
* 2 cups confectioners' sugar
* I tablespoon lemon juice
* I teaspoon pure vanilla extract

– Preheat the oven to 350°F. Spray three 9-inch baking pans with nonstick baking spray.

– In a large mixing bowl, using metal beaters, beat the butter, granulated sugar, and vanilla at medium speed until fluffy. Add the eggs, one at a time, beating well after each addition.

– In a medium bowl, combine the flour, baking soda, cinnamon, and salt. Add to the butter mixture alternately with the buttermilk, beginning and ending with the flour mixture and beating just until combined after each addition. Add the mashed bananas and pineapple, beating until combined.

– Using a measuring cup, spoon the batter into each of the three prepared pans, one scoop at a time to ensure an even distribution. Slam the pans against the counter to get any air bubbles out of the batter.

– Bake until a wooden pick inserted in the center comes out clean, 25 to 35 minutes. Cool in the pans for 10 minutes. Remove from the pans and cool completely on wire racks.

– Spread some frosting between the layers. Spread the remaining frosting over the top and sides of the cake. Garnish with coconut and nuts if desired.

Frosting:

– Beat the butter and cream cheese together with a handheld electric mixer until smooth and creamy. Beat in the confectioners' sugar in increments. Lastly beat in the lemon juice and vanilla.

Chapter 8: August

Summer winds down
First Quarter Moon of the Late Summer

* Blackened Shrimp with Cucumber Chow-Chow

* Sautéed Kale with Shallots and Malt Vinegar Reduction

* Sweet Potato Corn Bread

* Banana Tart

BLACKENED SHRIMP WITH CUCUMBER CHOW-CHOW

Makes 8 servings

* 2 pounds medium shrimp, peeled
* Chef Jesse's Spice blend (SEE PAGE 26 FOR RECIPE)
* Grape-seed oil

Too easy.

– Dredge shrimp in spice blend, then heat oil in a large skillet and cook until blackened on both sides, no more than 3-4 minutes.

CUCUMBER CHOW-CHOW

Makes 6 to 8 servings

* 6 cucumbers
* ¼ teaspoon EACH: sea salt and black pepper

* ½ lemon (juice and grated zest)
* 8-12 cherry tomatoes sliced in half
* ½ scotch bonnet pepper, no seeds (optional)
* 2 tablespoons cilantro, chopped
* 1 clove garlic, crushed
* ½ small red onion

- You can use any cucumber you have on hand, and the option to peel or not is totally up to you. Remember to wear gloves when handling scotch bonnet peppers and to wash your hands immediately after with soap and water.

- Cut the stems and bottoms off the cucumbers and cut into spears and place in a large bowl. I also use some cherry tomatoes, for added flavor, color, and texture. You can use any tomato you have.

- Crush or dice the garlic, chop the cilantro, and either dice the scotch bonnet or cut it into large pieces so that when you serve it, your guests can easily identify the pieces and avoid them if they wish. Top of Form

SAUTÉED KALE WITH SHALLOTS AND MALT VINEGAR REDUCTION

To make the reduction, boil ½ cup malt vinegar down to about 2 tablespoons.

Makes 8 servings

* ¼ cup extra-virgin olive oil
* 3 cloves garlic, smashed
* 2 cups shallots, minced
* 6 to 8 cups fresh kale, rinsed and drained
* ¼ cup vegetable stock

* ½ teaspoon kosher salt
* ¼ teaspoon freshly ground black pepper
* 2 tablespoons malt vinegar reduction*

- Remove stems from kale, then wash thoroughly and spin dry. Coarsely chop kale. In a large, heavy skillet, heat oil over medium-high heat. Cook and stir garlic and shallots for 2 minutes and stir in the kale to cook for 5 minutes. Reduce heat, stir in stock, cover and steam 10 minutes. Season to taste with salt, pepper, and malt vinegar reduction.

- Toss and serve hot.

SWEET POTATO CORN BREAD

Cook sweet potato in oven or microwave until soft, then cool, peel, and mash.

Makes 1 dozen

* 1-⅓ cups cake flour
* ⅔ cup cornmeal
* ⅔ cup granulated sugar
* ½ cup corn flour
* 1 tablespoon baking powder
* ½ teaspoon kosher salt
* 1⅓ cups buttermilk
* 5 tablespoons unsalted butter, melted
* 1 small sweet potato, cooked and mashed

- In a large bowl, combine flour, cornmeal, granulated sugar, corn flour, baking powder, and salt. Stir to mix. In a separate bowl, combine milk, butter, egg, and mashed sweet potato. Add to the dry ingredients and blend just until large lumps are dissolved.

- Pour mixture into a greased 8-inch-square baking pan or 10-inch cast-iron skillet. Bake at 350°F until done, about 25 minutes.

prick with a fork, then put cooked bananas over the pastry. Bake 30-40 minutes at 350°F or until golden. Cool and serve. Great with a scoop of vanilla ice cream.

BANANA TART

Makes 8 servings

* ½ cup (1 stick) unsalted butter
* 1 teaspoon ground cinnamon
* 1 cup packed dark brown sugar
* ½ cup banana liqueur
* 8 medium bananas, peeled and sliced

**Tart dough
(makes 2 tarts):**
* 5¼ cups pastry flour (or all-purpose)
* 2 teaspoons granulated sugar
* 1 tablespoon kosher salt
* 4 sticks cold unsalted butter, cut into small pieces
* 1 cup ice water

- Combine flour and salt into a bowl. Add butter and mix until it resembles coarse meal. Add ice water to form a dough. Wrap in plastic and refrigerate 1 hour.

- In a large skillet, melt butter, add cinnamon and brown sugar and stir, simmering over medium heat until the sugar dissolves, about 3 minutes. Add banana liqueur and blend well. Add sliced bananas and cook about 5-6 minutes or until soft.

- Roll pastry out on a lightly floured work surface. Line a 9-inch tart tin with pastry,

Aunt Minnie Mae Smothers It

* Smothered Chicken in Rosemary Gravy
* Homemade Papparadelle
* Chopped Salad
* Tiramisu

SMOTHERED CHICKEN IN ROSEMARY GRAVY

Aunt Minnie Mae was the master of smothered chicken. We all begged her to make it for family gatherings.

Makes 8 servings

* 2 2½ pound frying chickens, quartered
* 1½ cups all-purpose flour
* 1 teaspoon Chef Jesse Spice Blend (see pp 26)
* ½ cup grape-seed oil
* ½ medium yellow onion, peeled and diced
* 4 cups chicken stock
* 2 tablespoons chopped fresh rosemary

– Combine flour and spice blend in a bowl. Dredge chicken in seasoned flour, shaking off excess.

– In a Dutch oven, heat the oil over medium-high heat and fry the chicken in batches, about 5-6 minutes per side. Transfer to a plate when cooked.

– Add onion to the pan and sauté 1 minute. Add ½ cup reserved flour. Stir to make a roux and cook until fragrant and a lovely nut-brown color, about 5-7 minutes. Add stock, stirring constantly to make a smooth gravy. Season with rosemary and taste and adjust seasonings with salt and pepper.

- Return the chicken to the pan and simmer, covered, until the chicken is cooked through and tender (about ½ hour).

- Serve chicken with sauce over homemade pappardelle.

HOMEMADE PAPPARDELLE

Get out your pasta machine. This is easy. If you need a visual, just go to YouTube and see a video of pasta-making.

Makes enough for 8 servings

* 5 cups all-purpose flour, divided
* 1½ teaspoons sea salt, divided
* 6 large eggs, divided
* 6 large egg yolks, divided
* 6 tablespoons (or more) water, divided
* Pecorino cheese for dusting

- Place 2½ cups flour and ¾ teaspoon salt in processor; blend 5 seconds. Whisk 3 eggs, 3 yolks, and 3 tablespoons water in bowl.

- With machine running, pour egg mixture through feed tube. Blend until sticky dough forms, adding water by teaspoonful if dry.

- Scrape dough out onto floured work surface. Knead dough until smooth and no longer sticky, sprinkling lightly with flour as needed, about 8 minutes. Shape into ball. Cover with plastic wrap and let rest 45 minutes. Repeat with remaining flour, salt, eggs, yolks, and water.

- Divide each dough ball into 4 pieces. Cover dough with plastic wrap.

- Set pasta machine to widest setting. Flatten 1 dough piece into 3-inch-wide rectangle. Run through machine 5 times, dusting lightly with flour if sticking. Continue to run piece through machine, adjusting to next-narrower setting after every 5 passes, until dough is about 26 inches long. Cut crosswise into 3 equal pieces. Run each piece through machine, adjusting to next-narrower setting, until strip is a scant 1/16-inch thick and 14 to 16 inches long. Return machine to original setting for each piece. Arrange strips in a single layer on sheets of parchment.

- Repeat with remaining dough. Let strips stand until slightly dry to touch, 20 to 30 minutes. Fold strips in half so short ends meet, then fold in half again. Cut strips into ⅔-inch-wide pappardelle. DO AHEAD: *Can be made 1 day ahead. Arrange pappardelle in a single layer on sheets of parchment. Stack sheets in roasting pan. Cover and chill.*

- Bring a large pot of barely salted water to a boil, and cook the pasta until al dente no more than 5 minutes. Cool on a rack, then toss with butter. Dust with shredded Pecorino.

CHOPPED SALAD

Makes 8 servings

Dressing:

* ¼ cup red wine vinegar
* 1½ tablespoons finely chopped shallot
* ½ tablespoon honey
* ¼ cup hazelnut oil or extra-virgin olive oil

Salad:

* 6 cups chopped romaine hearts
* 4 cups sliced red cabbage
* 1 large Fuji apple, halved, cored, diced
* 1 Asian pear, halved, cored, diced
* 1 mango, peeled, diced
* ¾ cup hazelnuts, toasted, husked, coarsely chopped
* ½ cup pomegranate seeds
* ½ cup crumbled blue cheese (optional)

– Whisk dressing in a small bowl.

– Toss salad ingredients in a large salad bowl, then drizzle over dressing. Toss and serve.

TIRAMISU

Makes 8 servings

* 2 cups boiling water
* 3 tablespoons instant espresso powder
* ½ cup plus 1 tablespoon granulated sugar, divided
* 3 tablespoons Tia Maria (coffee liqueur)
* 4 large egg yolks
* ⅓ cup dry Marsala
* 1 pound mascarpone (2½ cups)

* 1 cup chilled heavy cream
* 36 *savoiardi* (crisp Italian ladyfingers; from 2 7-ounce packages)
* Unsweetened cocoa powder for dusting

– Stir together water, espresso powder, 1 tablespoon granulated sugar, and Tia Maria in a shallow bowl until sugar has dissolved, then cool.

– Beat egg yolks, Marsala, and remaining ½ cup granulated sugar in a metal bowl set over a saucepan of barely simmering water, using a whisk or handheld electric mixer until tripled in volume, 5 to 8 minutes. Remove bowl from heat. Beat in mascarpone until just combined.

– Beat cream in a large bowl until it holds stiff peaks.

– Fold mascarpone mixture into whipped cream gently but thoroughly.

– Dipping both sides of each ladyfinger into coffee mixture, line bottom of a 13 by 9 by 3 baking pan with 18 ladyfingers in 3 rows, trimming edges to fit if necessary. Spread half the mascarpone filling on top. Dip remaining 18 ladyfingers in coffee and arrange over filling in pan.

– Spread remaining mascarpone filling on top and dust with cocoa. Chill, covered, at least 6 hours.

– Let tiramisu stand at room temperature 30 minutes before serving. Dust with more cocoa.

Lobster, Lobster, everywhere You Look

Served up and down the East Coast, in diners large and small, the lobster pie is a good way to use up those little one-pounders known as chicken lobsters, and also a great way to celebrate summer when lobsters are at their peak.

In Maine, cooks crumble up crackers to make a crust, but Southern cooks know you will love a Southern pastry on top. Traditionally made and cooked for each person in oval ramekins, it's just a matter of cooking the lobsters in boiling water, then picking out the meat and dividing it among the ramekins. Plus, you can buy fresh cooked lobster meat in fishmonger shops too, and you don't even have to boil 'em up.

* Downhome Lobster Pie in a Southern Pastry Shell
* Red Rice Salad
* Summer Fruit Composé with Poppy Seed Dressing
* Panna Cotta with Fresh Seasonal Berries, Honey, and Mint

DOWNHOME LOBSTER PIE

Makes 8 servings

* ½ cup grape-seed oil
* ½ cup EACH: onions, carrots, celery, and leeks, chopped
* ⅓ cup garlic, minced
* ½ cup EACH: fresh thyme and tarragon
* 1 teaspoon EACH: white pepper and Old Bay Seasoning
* Sea salt to taste
* ½ cup all-purpose flour
* 4 cups seafood or lobster stock, heated to a boil
* 4 lobster tails, raw, medium dice
* 1 tablespoon brandy

- Heat the oil in a Dutch oven, then add the onions, carrots, celery, leeks, garlic and sauté until tender, about 5 minutes, stirring. Add thyme, tarragon, pepper, and Old Bay Seasoning.

- Add ½ cup oil. Stir in the flour to make a roux. Cook 3-5 minutes or until it is fragrant and a gorgeous nut-brown color.

- Add stock and brandy. Cook until thickened. Cool

- Add the raw lobster meat, mix into the blind baked shell. Add top layer of dough. Poke holes in dough.

- Bake 25 minutes.

*BASIC SOUTHERN PIE CRUST

Makes 1 double-crust pie, 2 single crusts, or six ramekins for pot pies

Single-Pie Crust

* 1 ½ cups all-purpose flour, chilled
* ½ cup lard or vegetable shortening, chilled
* ½ teaspoon kosher salt
* 4 to 8 tablespoons ice water

Double Pie Crust

* 2 cups all-purpose flour, chilled
* ⅔ cups lard or vegetable shortening, chilled
* ½ teaspoon kosher salt
* 5 to 10 tablespoons ice water

For ramekins, roll out a large rectangle, then place a ramekin on top and cut to the correct size; repeat and stack them with layers of parchment between layers while you make the filling. Place filling in each ramekin, then add the top and seal down using a little egg white for glue. Bake as directed at 350°F, about 20 minutes or so depending on the ramekin's size.

How to make pastry in the food processor:

Using the regular steel blade, place the flour, shortening, and salt in food processor and pulse 5 or 6 times until it looks mealy. With machine running, begin to add the water in a steady stream through the tube, just until dough begins to gather around the blade, about 10 seconds (don't over process). You may not need all the water—you don't want your dough to be wet or sticky to the touch. The dough should hold together when squeezed. If your dough is crumbly, it needs more water; add in a tablespoon at a time.

Remove dough from the machine, make a ball, and then press into a thick disc, like a giant burger—two discs if you made the double recipe. Wrap in plastic wrap and chill in the fridge for about 1 hour before rolling out. Can also be made several days in advance and stored in the fridge till needed, or frozen. Allow 2 to 3 hours for thawing before rolling out.

Roll the dough out on a lightly floured piece of waxed paper, and sprinkle a tiny bit of flour on top of the dough disc. Use a light forward motion only when rolling (don't rock the rolling pin back and forth—roll only in one direction) but periodically lift and turn the dough to prevent sticking and to keep it circular in shape. Add a bit more flour to the surface only if necessary. Roll out to about 2 inches larger than the pie plate, about ⅛ of an inch thick.

Gently roll the dough up around the rolling pin, or simply fold it over to make it easier to transport to the pie plate. Position and unroll or unfold, carefully molding from the inside of the pie plate to the edges. Trim excess dough with kitchen shears and either flute the edges by using the forefinger of one hand and pinching the dough next to it between your forefinger and thumb of the other hand and continuing around the crust, or simply take the rolling pin and roll firmly across the top to trim. Finish as directed in your recipe, as to pre-bake or not.

Blind Baking:

If your pie requires a pre-baked crust, dock the crust before baking using the tines of a fork to poke holes all around the bottom of the crust. This will prevent the crust from bubbling. You can also line the crust with parchment paper or aluminum foil and fill the foil with pie weights. Bake at 350 degrees for about 15 minutes. Remove paper or foil and cook another 5 minutes, or until crust is dry, but not browned. Allow crust to cool before filling and proceed with recipe.

RED RICE SALAD

Makes 6 to 8 servings

Find the Piedmont Italian red rice in high-end grocery stores everywhere. Such a brilliant ruby color, and it makes a perfect base for a summer rice salad.

* 1 cup Piedmont Italian red rice
* Sea salt and freshly grated black pepper to taste
* 2 tablespoons red wine vinegar
* 5 tablespoons extra-virgin olive oil, plus more for drizzling
* ¾ cup mixed, halved red and gold cherry tomatoes
* ½ cup corn kernels (about 1 ear)
* 4 ounces Asiago cheese, chopped (about ½ cup)
* ¼ cup EACH diced cucumber, radishes, and scallions
* ½ cup basil leaves, torn
* 4 teaspoons chopped flat-leaf parsley

— Bring a large pot of unsalted water to a boil. Add the rice and boil until the grains begin to split, 15 to 18 minutes. Salt the water heavily and cook until the grains are tender, 5 to 10 minutes longer. Drain the rice very well and spread it out on a large rimmed baking sheet. Drizzle with the vinegar and 2½ tablespoons of the olive oil. Let cool.

— Transfer the rice to a large bowl. Toss with the tomatoes, corn, cheese, cucumber, radishes, scallions, herbs, and the remaining 2½ tablespoons oil. Adjust seasonings with salt, pepper, and more vinegar to taste. Serve warm or chilled.

SUMMER FRUIT COMPOSÉ WITH POPPY SEED DRESSING

Makes 6 to 8 servings

This ad-lib salad is made with the freshest in-season fruits you see at the farmer's market and can change as the summer season progresses.

Arrange the bite-sized pieces of fruit on a flat platter. Serve with your own homemade poppy seed dressing on the side. (A gravy boat is ideal for this.)POW!

POPPY SEED DRESSING

* ½ cup grape-seed oil
* ¼ cup white balsamic vinegar
* ¼ cup granulated sugar
* I teaspoon poppy seeds
* I teaspoon Dijon mustard
* I teaspoon salt

– Stir together in a jar with a lid. Store in the refrigerator up to 2 weeks.

PANNA COTTA W/ FRESH SEASONAL BERRIES, HONEY, AND MINT

Such a great finish for a complicated meal. Make it ahead at your convenience.

Makes 6 servings

* I cup whole milk
* I cup heavy cream
* ½ cup granulated sugar
* 2 teaspoons gelatin

* I teaspoon vanilla extract

– In medium saucepan, heat milk, cream, and granulated sugar until the sugar is dissolved.

– Soften the gelatin in 1 cup cold water and add to the hot milk mixture. Stir until dissolved, and then mix in vanilla. Pour into 3- or 4-ounce buttered ramekins, and chill until set, about 6 hours or overnight.

– (I love to go to the farmer's market to see what seasonal fruits are on display and gather some for this recipe. Also jam works well. I like strawberries, blueberries, and blackberries to serve over panna cotta.)

– In a medium bowl, toss a few seasonal fruits with a bit of honey, a squeeze of lemon, and fresh mint. Once you have turned the panna cottas out onto dessert plates, top each one with fruit. POW!

A late-summer picnic for my mama's birthday

We all come out for my mama's party. Everybody brings their best dish. Oh, those ladies are competitive. But I just bring what I knows my mama likes best.

* Baby Kale Salad

* Herbed Oil Red Potato Salad

* Chef Jesse's Barbecued Pig's Feet

* Down-Home Coconut Cake

BABY KALE SALAD

Makes four servings

* 1 ½ tablespoons apple cider vinegar
* 2 tablespoons grape-seed oil
* 1 tablespoon honey
* ½ teaspoon kosher salt
* 5 ounces baby kale
* ¼ cup golden raisins
* 3 tablespoons toasted pecans
* Salt and fresh-ground black pepper

- Combine the vinegar, oil, honey, and salt in a small mason jar. Seal tightly and shake to combine. Place the kale in a large salad bowl. Just before serving, add the dressing, and toss to coat the kale.

- Add golden raisins and pecans and toss again.

- Season to taste with salt and pepper, serve quickly.

HERBED OIL RED POTATO SALAD

Makes four servings

* 1½ pounds red potatoes (about 15 diced medium)
* ½ cup minced fresh herbs (parsley, tarragon, chives)
* 2 scallions, sliced thin
* 1 tablespoon of whole grain mustard
* 1 tablespoon apple cider vinegar
* ½ cup diced gherkin pickles, minced fine
* ½ cup pimentos diced fine
* Kosher salt and black pepper to taste

– Fill a large pot of water and place potatoes in pot, cook for 12-14 minutes. Drain and air cool.

– In a medium bowl, mix the herbs, scallions, oil, mustard, vinegar, pickles, pepper, salt, and pepper. Adjust seasoning and toss with potatoes.

CHEF JESSE'S BBQ PIGS FEET

Makes 8 servings

* 8 fresh pig feet (about 5 pounds, split in half)

– Season with Chef Jesse's Spice Blend (see pp 26), rubbing all over pig feet. Marinate overnight in a covered dish in the refrigerator.

Next day:
* ½ cup EACH: grape-seed oil, diced carrots, celery, and onion
* 3 garlic cloves, smashed
* 2 quarts water AND apple cider vinegar

* 2 teaspoons crushed red pepper
* 1 tablespoon EACH: kosher salt, black pepper, and pickling spice
* 4 thyme sprigs
* 1 cinnamon stick
* 2 cups of Chef Jesse's BBQ sauce (see page 162)

– Preheat oven to 425°F.

– Place marinated pig feet in a roasting pan, roast for 25 minutes or until golden brown, then remove from pan onto a plate. In same pan, add oil and sauté the carrots, celery, and onions for 5 minutes. Add garlic, stir, and cook about a minute more. Add pig feet back in, cover with water and vinegar, bring to a boil, and add crushed pepper, salt, black pepper, pickling spice, thyme and cinnamon stick. Lower oven to 300°F. Cover pan with lid or foil and braise for 2½ hours or until tender. Strain braising liquid (this can make some great broth for greens).

– Sprinkle vegetables over the pig feet, cover with Chef Jesse's BBQ sauce, and bake for about 25 minutes more. Serve hot.

DOWN-HOME COCONUT CAKE

Makes 12 to 16 servings

– Preheat oven to 375°F. Grease and flour 3 9-inch round cake pans

* 3 cups cake flour
* 2½ teaspoons baking powder

* ½ teaspoon salt
* I cup (2 sticks) unsalted butter
* 2 cups granulated sugar
* 4 large eggs
* I cup milk
* I teaspoon lemon extract
* I teaspoon pure vanilla extract
* ½ teaspoon vegetable oil

Chef Jesse's pineapple filling

* Butter cream frosting
* ½ cup coconut flakes

— Combine the flour, baking powder, and salt in a bowl. In an electric mixer, cream together the butter and granulated sugar on medium speed until light. Add the eggs one at a time, beating well after each addition.

— Add the dry ingredients to the mixture, alternating with the milk and beginning and ending with flour mixture. Stir in the lemon, vanilla extract, and oil.

— Pour the batter into three prepared 9-inch round baking pans. Bake for 20 to 25 minutes. Insert wooden pick in the center of the cake to see if it comes out clean.

— Let the layers cool. Place the bottom layer on a cake plate and spread Chef Jesse's pineapple filling between the layers. Add a little frosting in between the layers, and sprinkle coconut. Repeat process until the cake is completely covered in frosting.

BUTTER CREAM FROSTING

Makes 4 cups

* I cup butter
* ½ cup shortening
* I cup granulated sugar
* 4 large egg whites
* ½ teaspoon fresh lemon juice
* ¾ teaspoon vanilla extract
* I tablespoon water (optional); for a softer butter cream, blend in the water

— In an electric mixer with paddle attachment, cream together the butter, shortening, and granulated sugar until well blended. Add the egg whites, lemon juice, and vanilla. Blend at medium speed, then mix at high speed until light and fluffy.

FRESH PINEAPPLE FILLING

Makes 2 cups

1 whole pineapple (peeled, cored, and crushed)
* ¼ cup granulated sugar

— In a saucepan, add the crushed pineapple and granulated sugar, bring to a boil, and cook for 5 minutes, or until pineapple is cooked through and juice becomes syrupy. Cool for cake later.

Chapter 9: September

Back to School and Other Fall Feasts

* Baby Back Ribs with Honey Barbecue Sauce
* Mom's Baked Beans with Molasses
* Braised Kale with Apples
* Down-Home 7-Up Pound Cake

BABY BACK RIBS WITH HONEY BARBECUE SAUCE

Makes 6 servings

We could call these rainy day ribs, since they can be baked in the oven and you don't even have to think about an umbrella over the outdoor grill. POW!

* ¼ cup paprika
* ½ teaspoon EACH: cayenne pepper, black and white pepper
* 2 teaspoons EACH: granulated garlic and onion
* 1 tablespoon EACH: brown sugar and smoked salt
* ½ cup EACH: water and cider vinegar
* 1 cup apple juice
* 2 pounds of baby back ribs, cleaned

– Mix all the spices above in a bowl. Add vinegar and water to form a paste. Rub the paste over the ribs, cover in plastic, and marinate overnight in the refrigerator.

Next day:
– Preheat the oven to 350°F.

Feast #28

– Roast ribs for 1 hour uncovered in a baking dish. Once the ribs have browned, add apple juice and cover them in foil to cook for 1½ more hours or until fork tender. Let rest for 10 minutes, brush on barbecue sauce, and brown for 5 minutes more. Keep hot.

HONEY BARBECUE SAUCE

* 1 tablespoon grape-seed oil
* 1 red onion, minced
* 1 medium garlic, minced
* 1 cup EACH: ketchup and chili sauce (Heinz 57)
* 2 teaspoons hot sauce or to taste (Frank's is good)
* ½ cup EACH: cider vinegar and apple juice
* 1 cup EACH: honey and water
* ¼ cup Creole mustard
* 1 tablespoon Worcestershire sauce
* ⅓ teaspoon fresh thyme
* Sea salt and freshly ground black pepper to taste

– In a heavy saucepan, add oil over medium heat, then cook onion and garlic until soft and translucent, about 5 minutes. Stir in ketchup, chili sauce, cider vinegar, apple juice, hot sauce, honey, water, Creole mustard, Worcestershire, thyme, salt and pepper.

– Stir together and heat over medium heat about 20 minutes. Rub some on the ribs. Serve remaining sauce in a gravy boat at the table.

MOM'S BAKED BEANS WITH MOLASSES

As long as you've got that oven cranking, you should add a side of my mom's baked beans. POW! Remember to soak those dried beans overnight in water to cover.

When my mom made these beans when I was a kid, they lasted our little family for days and days. Still my favorite.

* 2 pounds dried beans (navy, cannellini, black, or pinto beans)
* 1 bay leaf
* 2 smoked ham hocks
* 1 medium yellow onion peeled and finely chopped
* Sea salt and freshly milled black pepper to taste
* ½ teaspoon hot sauce (or to taste)
* 2 tablespoons yellow mustard
* ½ cup EACH: molasses and tomato ketchup
* ¼ cup brown sugar

– Rinse beans and place in a large bowl with water to cover. Soak overnight, then drain the beans and place in a 4-quart pot with a lid. Cover with cold water and raise to a boil. Reduce heat to low and simmer until the beans are tender, up to 2 hours, checking to make sure water remains just covering them by a couple of inches.

– Add ham hocks to simmering water in a second pot. Cook about 45 minutes, then add onion, garlic, salt, pepper, and hot sauce. Simmer about 15 to 20 minutes more so that the juices cook down to about ½ cup.

- Preheat oven to 350°F. Lightly oil a large 6-quart oven-proof bowl (or bean pot).

- Drain the cooked beans and add them to the bowl. Combine the mustard, molasses, ketchup and brown sugar. Pour over beans along with ham hocks and liquid and mix well. Place bean pot in the oven and cook, covered with a lid or foil, 3-4 hours, adding water as needed to maintain a thick soupy mix.

- Taste and adjust seasonings with additional salt and/or pepper as needed.

- About halfway through the cooking, remove the lid and turn the heat down to 300°F. Cook, checking from time to time so that it doesn't boil dry. Add water as needed.

BRAISED KALE WITH APPLES

When the fall gives you apples, pick from two or three varieties to create the most complex flavor in this gorgeous autumn kale dish.

Makes 6 to 8 servings

* ¼ cup extra-virgin olive oil
* 1 medium yellow onion, peeled and chopped
* 3 cloves garlic, minced
* 2 cups apples, cored and chopped (Granny Smiths, Empire, Braeburns, Gravensteins) Leave the skin on the apples for texture and interest
* 2 bunches fresh kale, stemmed, thoroughly washed, and chopped

* ½ cup chicken or vegetable stock
* Sea salt and freshly milled black pepper to taste
* 2 tablespoons malt vinegar

- In a large skillet or stockpot, add oil and then heat and brown onion, then garlic. Add apples and brown them. Add kale and begin to cook it down, turning often, and cook until soft. Add stock, salt and pepper, and vinegar. Add a lid and braise until the greens are totally limp and mixed with onion, garlic, and apples. About 20 minutes.

DOWN-HOME 7-UP POUND CAKE

When Mom began to make this cake, we thought it was some kind of magic trick. Now I know this secret method just gives me a great tender and flavorful cake. POW! And wow. Is this a keeper? Yes.

* 1½ cups butter
* 3 cups granulated sugar
* 5 eggs, at room temperature
* 3 cups cake flour
* 1 tablespoon lemon flavoring
* ¾ cup carbonated lemon-lime beverage (7-Up preferred)

- Preheat oven to 350°F. Grease/flour a tube or Bundt pan.

- Cream butter and granulated sugar together until light and fluffy.

- Add eggs one at a time, beating after each one.

- Add flour alternately with 7-Up. Stir in lemon flavoring.

- Bake in prepared pan until cake tests done, approximately an hour. Cool on a rack, then turn out onto a cake plate.

The Death of Zeus

My first word to Jesse was "NO!" And then, "No dogs. Who is going to take care of him, feed him, wash him, walk him?"

Well, I finally said yes and we got this wriggly little pup that our youngest son, Jesse, named Zeus: the god of all the gods, the god of sky and fire, the god of everything. Soon Zeus was the god that ran our house.

Zeus loved it when I cooked braised oxtails. I usually started late at night, after I came home from work. Zeus would lie in the kitchen door, raising his head and patting his tail as the sizzling went on. He would take deep breaths of that good food cooking. Zeus loved him some oxtails.

I would talk to him and tell him everything that had gone on that day. We were the only two up by then; me turning the oxtails, Zeus listening to every word I said. He looked up and I knew he understood. From time to time, I'd toss him a little scrap. You would have thought I'd given that dog a filet mignon. He was so grateful.

I am writing this down with tears pouring out of my eyes. Yes, I have heard some people say, "It's just a dog, get another one." But Zeus has been in our lives for 7 years. He is family. He was the smallest in the bunch, but grew up to be the biggest. I never thought he would die.

I didn't know how hard it would be to miss him so much. Things will never be the same because I'm so used to him greeting me when I come home. Before I could even put the keys in the door, he was barking.

I miss that barking now. After a while you get to understand your dog, and he understands you. Zeus had his good days and his bad days. In my mind, I would reminisce about the good times. For example, when we gave Zeus a bath, he hated to be wet and would run all over the house trying to dry himself off. That's a classic memory I will cherish for life.

POW! I think one of the reasons I hurt so bad is that when Jesse was in college for two years, I walked Zeus, fed him, and we became friends all over again.

When Zeus first started to limp, we took him to the doctor. The doctor said it was arthritis. We were relieved. Then Zeus started to get worse. Next visit, cancer was the word. We heard that some others in his family had it before him.

We all were devastated. He just got worse. Everyone told us we were letting him suffer, and we knew that wasn't right. But we hated to let him go. But finally, we took him back to the doctor to start his journey on the Rainbow Bridge.

We all sat in that room with him a long time after he was gone. It was so hard to leave that room.

I think now we did the right thing, He wasn't living a healthy life. He couldn't run, couldn't have a good time. Soon, he was bleeding from the nose every day. And we could see the pain in his eyes. He was crying and suffering, and we were the witnesses who were watching him deteriorate day by day. As we watched Zeus take his last breath on that fateful day, I had a sense of guilt. Why couldn't I save him?

I cried so hard, and everything flashed in my mind. Zeus was human to us. He was family. We will never forget him. No other dog will take his place.

Yes, we had our ups and downs, but Zeus was always right there with us. How can we go on without him? How can we face all that life throws at us without our Zeus?

REST IN PEACE, ZEUS. Have fun running up and down that Rainbow Bridge in Heaven. No more pain. No more suffering. And a big old dinner every night. Please cook this feast in memory of our dog ZEUS! And good dogs everywhere. POW!

Oxtails Low and Slow

* Chef Jesse's Braised Oxtails with Callaloo

* Classic Risotto

* Old Fashioned Scratch Lemon Meringue Pie

BRAISED OXTAILS WITH CALLALOO

Makes 6 to 8 servings

This is one of those all day and dinner on the grounds recipes. Cook it low and slow. Not too hard to do, just takes patience.

CHEF JESSE'S BRAISED OXTAILS

Makes 4 to 6 servings

* 5 pounds of beef oxtails (fat removed, washed)
* *Chef Jesse's Spice Blend*
    * I teaspoon kosher salt
    * ½ teaspoon EACH: black pepper and white pepper
    * I teaspoon EACH: granulated garlic, onion, and paprika
* ½ cup + 2 cups grape-seed oil, divided
* 4 medium carrots, peeled and cut medium dice
* I medium onion, cut into medium dice
* 4 celery stalks, cut into medium dice
* ½ cup tomato paste
* 2 cups dry red wine (pinot is great)
* 4 cups beef broth (homemade or store-bought)
* 6 to 8 sprigs fresh thyme

Prepare Oxtails

– In a bowl, add oxtails to Chef Jesse's blend with ½ cup oil. Mix well, cover, and marinate overnight.

Next day:

– Preheat the oven to 375°F.

– In a large oven-proof saucepan, heat 2 tablespoons oil over medium-high heat until just smoking. Sear the oxtails on all sides, then remove them, add carrots and onions to the pan, and sauté for 2 minutes. Add celery, stirring quickly.

– Add tomato paste and cook for 2 minutes more. Add wine to deglaze pan, plus stock, bay leaf, and thyme. Now raise the heat to high and bring to a boil, stirring and scraping the bottom. Add oxtails back to the saucepan, cover and place in the oven, and bake until tender, about 2 to 2½ hours at 300°F.

– Remove the oxtails to a platter. Skim off fat from the pan, bring to a boil, reduce by one-third, then add oxtails. Give it one big stir and then serve over rice. POW!

CALLALOO

This Trinidadian green is full-flavored and full of minerals. POW!

Makes 6 to 8 servings

* 2 pounds callaloo (substitute Swiss chard or mustard greens)
* 1 tablespoon cooking oil
* 1 tablespoon butter
* 1 onion, chopped
* 3 whole scallions, chopped
* 1 sprig fresh thyme, or ½ teaspoon dried
* ½ teaspoon salt
* ½ teaspoon freshly ground black pepper
* ⅓ cup water

– Remove the small branches with leaves from the main stem and submerge the callaloo in a bowl of cold water. Let soak for a minute and remove, discarding the water. Repeat 2 more times. Finely chop the leaves and branches and set aside.

– Heat the oil and butter in a medium-size skillet over medium heat until the butter is melted. Add the onion and scallions, stirring until the onion begins to soften, about 2 minutes. Add the callaloo, thyme, salt, and black pepper. Mix all the ingredients together, add the water, and cover. Cook over medium heat until the stems are tender, about 8 minutes.

CLASSIC RISOTTO

Makes 6 to 8 servings

* 5½ cups chicken stock, preferably homemade
* 2 tablespoons extra-virgin olive oil
* 1 small onion, finely chopped
* Sea salt and freshly ground black pepper
* 1½ cups Arborio rice (10 ounces)
* Pinch of saffron threads
* ½ cup dry white wine
* ½ cup freshly grated Parmigiano-Reggiano cheese

* 1 tablespoon unsalted butter
* 2 tablespoons chopped flat-leaf parsley

— In a medium saucepan, bring the chicken stock to a simmer; keep warm. In a large saucepan, heat the olive oil. Add the onion, season with salt and pepper, and cook over moderate heat, stirring until softened, about 5 minutes. Add the rice and cook for 1 minute, stirring to thoroughly coat. Crumble the saffron into the wine and add it to the rice. Cook, stirring until the wine is absorbed. Add 1 cup of the warm stock and cook over moderate heat, stirring constantly until nearly absorbed. Continue adding the stock ½ cup at a time, stirring constantly until it is nearly absorbed between additions. The risotto is done when the rice is al dente and suspended in a thick, creamy sauce, about 20 minutes total. Season the risotto with salt and pepper to taste. Stir in the cheese, butter, and parsley and serve immediately.

OLD FASHIONED SCRATCH LEMON MERINGUE PIE

Makes 8 servings

So much more flavorful than a pie that starts in a box. This is the real deal, full of great lemon flavor and a gorgeous pastry you made yourself. POW!

For the pastry. Makes 2 10-inch pie shells:

* 1 cup very cold butter cut into small cubes
* 2½ cups all-purpose or pastry flour
* ½ tsp sea salt

* ¼ cup to ⅓ ice water (only enough to make a dough form)

For the filling:
* ⅓ cup corn starch
* ⅓ cup cake flour
* pinch sea salt
* 1½ cups granulated sugar
* 5 egg yolks, slightly beaten
* zest of 2 lemons, very finely chopped
* juice of 2 lemons
* 2 cups water
* 3 tablespoons unsalted butter

For the meringue:
* 5 large egg whites
* 1¼ cups granulated sugar
* ¼ teaspoon cream of tartar
* pinch sea salt
* 1 teaspoon vanilla extract

To make the pastry:

— Using a food processor or a pastry blender cut cold butter into flour and salt until mixture resembles a coarse meal. Small pieces of butter should still be visible.

— Pour cold water over the mixture and work in by tossing with a fork until dough begins to form. Use your hands as little as possible and work the dough as little as possible.

— Divide dough into 2 balls. Flatten into 2 rounds, wrap in plastic wrap, and place in the refrigerator to rest for a minimum of 20 minutes. You can freeze the second round for another time, but make sure you take it out of the fridge for 10 minutes to warm slightly before rolling out.

- Roll the dough into a 12-inch round and place in the bottom of a 10-inch pie plate.

- Trim and flute the edges as desired. Poke a few holes in the bottom of the pastry shell, and rest in the refrigerator for an additional 20 minutes before baking at 400 degrees F for 12 to 15 minutes or until golden brown.

- Cool completely before adding the filling.

To make the filling:

- In a medium saucepan, combine corn starch, cake flour, granulated sugar and salt. Pour in water and stir constantly over medium-low heat until mixture comes to a slow boil.

- Remove the pan from the heat and reduce the flame to low. Pour about a cup of this mixture onto the slightly beaten egg yolks while whisking constantly.

- Pour the egg mixture back into the rest of the other mixture in the pot, whisking constantly. Return to the stove and cook for an additional 3 minutes, stirring constantly.

- Remove from heat and stir in lemon juice and lemon zest. Finally whisk in butter one tablespoon at a time.

- Pour the filling into the baked and cooled shell. Let stand for a few minutes while preparing the meringue.

To prepare the meringue:

- Whip egg whites, vanilla, salt, and cream of tartar to soft peaks. Very gradually add the granulated sugar while continuing to beat the egg whites.

- Dollop in heaping tablespoonfuls onto pie. Gently spread over the filling, making sure that the meringue touches the crust all the way around the pie. This will help to prevent the meringue from shrinking.

- Bake in a 325°F oven for 20 to 25 minutes or until the meringue is well browned. Cool pie thoroughly in the refrigerator before serving.

- Dip a sharp knife in cold water to help with cutting the pie into slices, and clean the knife with paper towel between cuts.

Easy Etoufee

* Shrimp Etouffee with Jasmine Rice
* Corn Flat Break with Scallions and Shredded Cheddar Crust
* Autumn Fruit Salad
* White Blondies

SHRIMP ETOUFFEE WITH JASMINE RICE

Makes 8 servings

* Chef Jesse's Seasoning Mix
    * 2 teaspoons EACH: sea salt and cayenne pepper
    * I teaspoon EACH: white pepper, black pepper, and dried sweet basil
    * ½ teaspoon dried thyme

– Mix and store in a jar in a cool, dark place.

* 7 tablespoons grape-seed oil
* ½ cup EACH: chopped onions, celery, and green bell pepper
* 2 cloves garlic, minced
* ½ cup all-purpose flour
* 3 cups seafood or vegetable stock
* I cup unsalted butter (2 sticks)
* 2 pounds medium shrimp, peeled
* I cup green onions, finely chopped

– Stir seasonings mix into a jar. Preheat a large Dutch oven over medium heat. Add oil, onions, celery, and pepper. Cook and stir until tender, about 5 minutes. Add garlic and cook another minute, stirring.

– Stir flour into the mixture and cook and stir to make a golden roux, over medium heat. Continue cooking until it's a gorgeous nutty brown color.

- Add shrimp and seasonings mixture to the roux. Cook until the shrimp turn pink. About 5 minutes. Add stock, butter, and green onion. Simmer over low heat about 15 minutes.

- Serve over grits or rice.

JASMINE RICE

- Cook rice with barely salted water, 1 cup rice to 4 cups water. Cover until rice is cooked through, about 20 minutes. Toss with a fork.

CORN FLAT BREAD WITH SCALLIONS AND SHREDDED CHEDDAR CRUST

Makes 1 10-inch black skillet full to cut into thin wedges

* 1⅓ cups all-purpose flour
* 1 cup coarse stone-ground yellow cornmeal
* 2 teaspoons baking powder
* 1 teaspoon sea salt
* Pinch fresh-ground black pepper
* 1¼ cups whole milk
* 2 tablespoons honey
* 2 large eggs, beaten
* ⅓ cup + 1 tablespoon grape-seed oil, divided
* 1 green onion, white and tender green parts only, thinly sliced
* ½ cup shredded sharp cheddar

- Preheat the oven to 400°F.

- Place a 10-inch cast-iron skillet in the oven to heat.

- In a medium bowl, whisk the flour, cornmeal, baking powder, salt and pepper. In a small bowl, whisk the milk, honey, eggs and 1/3 cup of the oil. Add the wet ingredients to the cornmeal mixture and whisk just until combined. Stir in the scallions.

- Add the remaining 1 tablespoon of oil to the hot skillet and swirl to coat.

- Pour the batter into the skillet and bake for about 30 minutes, until the top is golden and a toothpick inserted in the center comes out clean. Top with shredded cheddar. Serve from the black skillet.

AUTUMN FRUIT SALAD

Makes about 6 to 8 servings

* 1½ pounds mixed citrus fruit (such as oranges, grapefruit, pomelo, tangerines, and mandarins), peeled and cut into segments, juices reserved separately
* ¼ cup mayonnaise
* 1 tablespoon juice + zest from 1 lemon
* 1 tablespoon honey
* 2 tablespoons extra-virgin olive oil
* Sea salt and freshly ground black pepper
* 1 Belgian endive
* 1 small head radicchio (about 5 ounces)
* 1 head escarole, washed and roughly chopped (about 6 cups)
* 1 large bulb fennel (about 6 ounces), shaved on a mandoline or fine cut with a very sharp knife

- Combine ¼ cup citrus juice with

mayonnaise and lemon juice in a medium bowl (save remaining citrus juice for another use). Whisk in honey. Whisking constantly, slowly add olive oil in a thin, steady stream. Season to taste with salt and pepper.

– Toss endive, radicchio, escarole, fennel, and citrus segments in a large bowl. Drizzle in half of dressing. Season to taste with salt and pepper, toss to combine, then drizzle in more dressing to taste. Serve immediately.

sprinkle with white chocolate chips.

– Bake in the preheated oven until a toothpick inserted into the center of the pan comes out clean, 30 to 35 minutes. Allow to cool in pan for about 10 minutes before cutting into bars.

⤜⤜⤜⟩⟨⤛⤛⤛

WHITE BLONDIES

Makes 8 generous servings

* 1 cup unsalted butter
* 4 (1 ounce) squares white chocolate, chopped
* 3 large eggs
* 2 cups granulated sugar
* 1 teaspoon vanilla extract
* 2 cups all-purpose flour
* 1 teaspoon sea salt
* 1 cup white chocolate chips

– Preheat oven to 350°F.

– Grease a 9 x 13 baking pan. Mix the butter and white chocolate together over low heat in a saucepan. Remove from heat, and let cool slightly. Meanwhile beat eggs with granulated sugar and vanilla extract in a mixing bowl. Mix in the butter mixture, and stir in the flour and salt until thoroughly combined. Scoop the batter into the prepared baking pan;

Chapter 10: October

Autumn sets in with all the football games and celebrations, including the biggest and best for this time of year: Halloween, now the second most celebrated holiday of the year. Time for a great feast. POW!

Friday Night Football Dinner

* Apple Cider Brined Pork Tenderloin with Honey BBQ Sauce
* Roasted Sweet Potato Mash with Candied Pecans
* Smothered Peppered Cabbage
* Applejack Bundt Cake with a Caramel Sauce

APPLE CIDER BRINED PORK TENDERLOIN WITH HONEY BBQ SAUCE

You want to talk about delicious? Pork tenders with my own honey BBQ sauce. POW!

Makes 6 to 8 servings

* 4 to 6 pork tenderloins

Brine:
* 1 cup apple cider
* ½ cup EACH: apple cider vinegar and brown sugar
* 2 teaspoons kosher salt
* 1 garlic clove, crushed
* 1 teaspoon EACH: mustard seeds and whole black peppercorns
* 5 sprigs fresh thyme
* 1 teaspoon fresh ginger, chopped

— Cook brine ingredients in a large pot until dissolved. Remove from the heat and add a couple of ice cubes to speed up the cooling. Add pork tenders, cover, and refrigerate overnight.

— Next day: Preheat the oven to 350°F. Season pork tenders to taste with salt and pepper. Film the bottom of a sauté pan with grape-seed oil, then brown meat on all sides, about 2 minutes. Transfer to the oven and cook about 10 minutes more.

Serve with:

CHEF JESSE'S HONEY BBQ SAUCE

* 1 tablespoon grape-seed oil
* 1 medium red onion, peeled and minced
* 1 clove garlic, minced
* 1 cup EACH: ketchup and chili sauce
* ½ cup EACH: apple juice and cider vinegar
* ⅓ cup (or to taste) hot sauce
* 1 cup EACH: honey and water
* ¼ cup Creole mustard
* 1 tablespoon Worcestershire sauce
* ⅓ teaspoon fresh thyme, minced
* 1 teaspoon coarse ground black pepper

— Sea salt and freshly milled black pepper to taste

— In a heavy saucepan, add oil over medium heat, then add onion and garlic and cook until clear and tender. About five minutes. Stir in ketchup, chili sauce, cider vinegar, hot sauce, honey, water, Creole mustard, Worcestershire sauce, thyme, salt and pepper. Bring to a boil, reduce heat, and simmer about 20 minutes. Adjust seasonings. POW! Transfer to a clear glass jar with a lid, and store in the refrigerator.

— This BBQ sauce is great with all meats.

ROASTED SWEET POTATO MASH WITH CANDIED PECANS

— Choose one sweet potato for each diner. Roast them in a 350°F oven until tender. About 1 hour.

— Let them cool, then peel and smash them in a large bowl using a stick blender. Season to taste with salt, pepper, and butter. Stir in candied pecans:

* 1 cup pecan halves
* 1 cup granulated sugar

— Mix pecans and granulated sugar together in an oven-proof dish. Cook in the oven until golden brown and glistening. POW!

SMOTHERED PEPPERED CABBAGE

My cousin Velma is the Queen of Peppered Cabbage, but I tried to squeeze mine right up there against hers. POW!

* ¼ cup bacon, chopped
* 1 teaspoon grape-seed oil
* 2 heads savoy cabbage, cut into thin slices
* 1 medium EACH: yellow onion, red and green bell peppers, seeded and chopped
* 1 tablespoon cider vinegar
* 1 teaspoon EACH: granulated sugar and Chef Jesse's spice blend (SEE PAGE 26 FOR RECIPE)
* 1 cup turkey or chicken stock

— In a large stewpot, cook the bacon with oil over medium heat until limp, then add cabbage, onion, and pepper. Cook and stir about 15 minutes, then add vinegar, stock, and essence to taste. Simmer about 5 more minutes, then correct seasonings and serve hot.

APPLEJACK BUNDT CAKE WITH A CARAMEL SAUCE

Makes 8 servings

* 4 cups thinly peeled, cored, and sliced Granny Smith apples
* ½ cup golden raisins
* ¼ cup applejack brandy
* 2 cups all-purpose flour
* ¾ teaspoon sea salt
* 1 tablespoon cinnamon
* 1 teaspoon mace
* 1½ teaspoons baking soda
* 3 large eggs
* 1 cup vegetable oil
* 2 cups granulated sugar
* 2 teaspoons vanilla extract
* ¾ cup pecan pieces

— Preheat the oven to 350°F. Grease a Bundt pan generously with butter and dust with flour.

— Soak apples and raisins in applejack for about 10 minutes. Meanwhile, sift flour, salt, cinnamon, mace together and set aside.

— Use electric mixer with the paddle and combine eggs and oil, then mix, and now blend in granulated sugar and vanilla. Beat until creamy. Gradually add flour and beat until completely mixed. Fold in apples and raisins. Transfer to the Bundt pan, pop into hot oven, and bake until done and a toothpick comes out clean, about 45-55 minutes.

CARAMEL SAUCE

* 1 packed cup brown sugar
* ½ cup half-and-half
* 4 tablespoons butter
* Pinch sea salt
* 1 tablespoon vanilla extract

— Mix the brown sugar, half-and-half, butter, and salt in a saucepan over medium-low heat. Cook while whisking gently for 5 to 7 minutes, until it gets thicker. Add the vanilla and cook another minute to thicken further. Turn off the heat, cool slightly, and pour the sauce into a jar. Refrigerate until cold.

— Drizzle over pieces of cake. POW!

Southern Fried Quail

* Southern Fried Quail
* Savannah Red Rice
* Low and Slow Southern Braised Collards
* Fall Clafoutis with Pears and Apples

SOUTHERN FRIED QUAIL

Quail hunting season varies from state to state but usually begins mid-October and ends in February. We like to have one big blow-out dinner sometime during this late fall period. That quail is really special. POW! Marinate the birds overnight for best results.

Makes 6-8 servings

* 6-12 whole picked and cleaned quail
* 1 cup buttermilk
* Pinch hot sauce

— Marinate overnight in a covered container in the refrigerator.

— Next day, make up this seasoned flour

  * 1 cup all-purpose flour
  * 1 teaspoon Lawry's seasoning
  * ½ teaspoon black pepper
  * ½ teaspoon cayenne pepper

— Lift the quail out of the buttermilk. Dredge in seasoned flour. Shake to remove excess flour.

— Heat 1-inch grape-seed oil in a heavy black cast iron skillet to 375°F. Fry quail until brown on both sides. Drain on a rack. Drain off all but 1 cup fat from the pan.

*To make gravy, simply add leftover flour mixture to the fat and stir to cook the flour, then add 2 cups chicken stock and cook and stir to make gravy, adjusting seasonings with salt and pepper. Serve in a gravy boat.

SAVANNAH RED RICE

* 1 cup EACH: onion, red and green bell pepper chopped
* 2 tablespoons butter
* 1 cup smoked sausage, diced
* 1 (14.5 ounce) can crushed tomatoes, with juice
* 1 tablespoon hot sauce
* 1 cup tomato sauce
* 1 cup chicken broth
* Sea salt, to taste
* Freshly milled black pepper to taste
* 1 cup uncooked long grain white rice

— Preheat oven to 350°F. In a saucepan over medium heat, sauté onion and bell pepper in butter. Add sausage; heat until mixture is slightly browned. Add tomatoes, hot sauce, tomato sauce and chicken broth. Season with pepper and salt as needed. Stir in rice. Pour mixture into a greased casserole and bake for 45 minutes.

LOW AND SLOW SOUTHERN BRAISED COLLARDS

Makes 6-8 servings

* 1 applewood smoked bacon slice, chopped
* ½ teaspoon crushed red pepper
* ¼ teaspoon salt
* 2 (16-ounce) package prewashed torn collard greens (or 3 bunches)
* 1 cup fat-free, less-sodium chicken broth
* ½ cup water
* ¼ cup dry white wine
* 1½ tablespoons cider vinegar

— Cook bacon in a Dutch oven over medium heat until crisp. Add pepper, salt, and greens; cook 2 minutes or until greens begin to wilt, stirring constantly. Stir in broth, water, wine and vinegar. Cover, reduce heat, and simmer 1 hour or until greens are tender.

FALL CLAFOUTIS WITH PEARS AND APPLES

The go-to dessert in France is basically a custard with fruits of the season. Swap out fruits for what you find in the farmer's market. Cherries are the classic. POW!

Makes 6 to 8 servings

* 1 cup whole milk
* 3 large eggs
* ½ cup granulated sugar
* 1 teaspoon vanilla extract
* 2 tablespoons butter, melted
* ½ cup all-purpose flour
* 1 large pear and/or apple, seeded and cut

into pieces

*   2 tablespoons Pear Au de Vie or Calvados

—   Preheat the oven to 325°F. In a large bowl, whisk together the milk, eggs, granulated sugar, vanilla, and butter until the sugar is dissolved. Add the flour and whisk until smooth. Pour the batter into a cast-iron skillet or pie pan.

—   Now add fruits. Cherries are the traditional French choice. But use your favorite fruit or flavoring. Bake until the clafoutis is beautifully puffed and golden, 35–40 minutes. Serve immediately.

Halloween Jambalaya For All

✳ Halloween Chicken and Sausage Jambalaya

✳ Jalapeño Cheddar Mini Corn Muffins

✳ Autumn Roasted Beet Salad with Apples

✳ Spiced Pumpkin Cake with Cream Cheese Pumpkin Frosting

HALLOWEEN CHICKEN AND SAUSAGE JAMBALAYA

Make this in the Crockpot or in a big stew pot on the back of the stove; then you'll have plenty of time to greet the trick-or-treaters as they come to the door.

* 12 ounces applewood-smoked bacon, diced
* 1 pound EACH: smoked fully cooked sausage (such as linguiça), halved lengthwise, cut crosswise into ½-inch-thick semicircles, and andouille
* ½ pound tasso or smoked ham (such as Black Forest), cut into ½-inch cubes
* 4 large yellow onions, peeled and chopped
* 2 large celery stalks, chopped
* 1 EACH: red and green bell pepper, coarsely chopped
* 6 large skinless boneless chicken thighs, cut into 1-inch pieces
* 2 tablespoons paprika
* 1 tablespoon EACH: chopped fresh thyme and chili powder
* ¼ teaspoon (or to taste) cayenne pepper
* 3 10-ounce cans diced tomatoes and green chiles
* 2½ cups beef broth + 1 cup water
* 2 cups long-grain white rice
* 2 cups green onions, chopped
* Chopped fresh Italian parsley all at

– Position rack in bottom third of oven and preheat to 350°F.

- Cook bacon in very large pot over medium-high heat until brown but not yet crisp, stirring often, for 8 to 10 minutes. Add smoked sausage, andouille, and tasso. Sauté until meats start to brown in spots, about 10 minutes. Add onions, celery, and bell peppers. Cook until vegetables begin to soften, stirring occasionally, 10 to 12 minutes. Mix in chicken. Cook until outside of chicken turns white, stirring often, 5 to 6 minutes. Mix in paprika, thyme, chili powder, and ¼ teaspoon cayenne. Cook 1 minute. Add diced tomatoes with chiles, broth, and water. Stir to blend well. Add more cayenne, if desired. Mix in rice.

- Bring jambalaya to boil. Cover pot. Place in oven and bake until rice is tender and liquids are absorbed, about 45 minutes. Uncover the pot. Mix chopped green onions into jambalaya; sprinkle with chopped parsley and serve.

JALAPEÑO CHEDDAR MINI CORN MUFFINS

* 6 tablespoons melted butter
* 2 cups stone ground cornmeal
* I cup all-purpose flour
* I tablespoon baking powder
* ½ teaspoon baking soda
* I teaspoon salt
* 3 large eggs
* 2 cups buttermilk
* 4 slices bacon, cooked and crumbled
* 2-3 tablespoons finely chopped jalapeño, seeds discarded
* ½ cup shredded cheddar

- Preheat the oven to 350°F.

- Mix all of the ingredients together with a whisk. Generously spray a mini muffin tin with nonstick spray. Fill the muffin tins almost to the top. Bake for about 15-20 minutes or until the tops spring back when touched. Turn out on a rack to cool.

AUTUMN ROASTED BEET SALAD WITH APPLES AND PEARS

Best time of year to enjoy root vegetables with freshly harvested fruits.

* ¾ pound golden beets, trimmed and cut into ¾-inch wedges
* ½ pound EACH: red apples and pears, cored and cut into ¾-inch wedges
* 2 tablespoons extra-virgin olive oil
* Sea salt to taste
* 4 cups mixed sturdy winter greens (such as baby kale, tatsoi, endive, and radicchio), torn or cut into bite-size pieces
* ⅓ cup crumbled fresh goat cheese
* ¼ cup toasted chopped pecans
* 3 tablespoons dried cherries

For the vinaigrette

* ¼ cup grape-seed oil
* ⅓ cup thinly sliced shallots
* Sea salt
* ½ teaspoon chopped fresh ginger
* 2 tablespoons balsamic vinegar
* I tablespoon pure maple syrup
* Juice and grated zest of one lime
* I teaspoon finely chopped fresh flat-leaf parsley

* 1 teaspoon Dijon mustard
* Freshly ground black pepper

Roast the beets and fruit

– Position racks in the upper and lower thirds of the oven and heat the oven to 450°F.

– In a large bowl, toss the beets with 1 tablespoon of the oil and ½ teaspoon salt. Transfer to a large-rimmed heavy-duty baking sheet. Spread into a single layer.

– In another large bowl, combine the apples and pears with the remaining 1 tablespoon of oil and another ½ teaspoon salt. Transfer to a large-rimmed heavy-duty baking sheet. Spread into a single layer.

– Roast, flipping with a spatula halfway through and rotating the baking sheets until browned and tender, 20 to 25 minutes. Let cool for a few minutes on the sheets. Transfer to a large bowl.

Make the vinaigrette

– Heat the oil in an 8-inch skillet over medium heat. Add the shallots and a pinch of salt and cook, stirring occasionally until softened and lightly browned, 2 to 4 minutes. Add the ginger and cook, stirring until fragrant and softened, about 15 seconds. Remove from the heat. Let the oil cool for 3 to 5 minutes.

– Meanwhile, in a small heatproof bowl, whisk the vinegar, maple syrup, lime juice, zest, parsley, mustard, ¼ teaspoon salt, and several grinds of fresh pepper. Whisk the warm oil into the vinegar mixture until emulsified.

– Season to taste, adding more lime juice, salt, or pepper as needed.

Assemble the salad

– Lightly season the greens with salt and then drizzle with 2 tablespoons of the warm vinaigrette. Toss, taste, and add a little more dressing, if necessary. Arrange the greens on a platter.

– Season the roasted beets and fruit with a pinch more salt, and dress them lightly with a bit of the remaining vinaigrette. Scatter over the greens, then top with the goat cheese, pecans, and cherries. Serve right away, passing the remaining dressing at the table.

SPICED PUMPKIN CAKE WITH CREAM CHEESE PUMPKIN FROSTING

Makes 12 servings

The cake can be made up to 2 days in advance. Refrigerate until cold, and then carefully cover with plastic wrap. The cake can also be wrapped tightly and frozen for up to 1 month. Let thaw in the refrigerator, about 12 hours.

* Butter for coating cake pans, at room temperature
* 2 cups all-purpose flour, plus extra for dusting the pan
* 2 cups granulated sugar
* 2 teaspoons EACH: baking soda and cinnamon
* 1 teaspoon sea salt
* ½ teaspoon freshly grated nutmeg

* ¼ teaspoon ground cloves
* 3 large eggs, beaten
* I cup vegetable oil
* 2 teaspoons pure vanilla extract
* I¼ cups canned unsweetened pumpkin purée
* I cup lightly packed sweetened flaked coconut
* ¾ cup canned crushed pineapple (do not drain)
* ⅓ cup dried currants

CREAM CHEESE PUMPKIN FROSTING

* 2 packages (8 ounces each) cream cheese, at room temperature
* I cup (2 sticks) unsalted butter, at room temperature
* 2 tablespoons canned unsweetened pumpkin purée
* I½ cups confectioners' sugar, sifted
* I teaspoon pure vanilla extract

— Position a rack in the center of the oven and preheat to 350°F. Butter two 9-inch diameter cake pans with 1½-inch sides. Line the bottom of each pan with a circle of parchment paper. Butter the parchment paper. Sprinkle the pans with flour, tap the pans to evenly distribute the flour, and then shake off the excess flour. Set aside.

— To make the cake, in a large bowl, sift together 2 cups flour, granulated sugar, baking soda, cinnamon, salt, nutmeg, and cloves. In a medium bowl, combine the eggs, oil, and vanilla. In another medium bowl, combine the pumpkin purée, coconut, crushed pineapple, and currants.

— Add the egg mixture to the flour mixture and stir with a wooden spoon until just combined. Add the pumpkin mixture and stir just until combined. Divide the batter between the prepared pans, spreading it evenly. Bake for 35 to 40 minutes until a toothpick inserted into the center of a cake comes out clean. Transfer to wire racks and let cool in the pans for 15 minutes. Run a table knife around the edge of the pans to loosen the cakes. Invert the cakes onto the racks and peel off the parchment paper. Let cool completely before frosting the cakes.

— To make the frosting, in the bowl of an electric mixer fitted with the paddle attachment, beat the cream cheese on medium speed for about 3 minutes until smooth. Add the butter and beat for about 2 minutes until combined. Add the pumpkin purée and beat until incorporated, about 1 minute. Add the confectioners' sugar and vanilla and beat for about 3 minutes until fluffy.

— Place 1 cake layer on a cake plate or platter. Using an offset spatula, spread half of the frosting over the top of the first cake layer. Spread the frosting right to the edge of the top without frosting the sides of the cake. Carefully place the second cake on top, lining up the edges. Spread the remaining frosting over the top of the cake without frosting the sides. Swirl the frosting to decorate the top. Refrigerate the cake to set the frosting. Remove from the refrigerator 30 to 40 minutes before serving.

November: Chapter 11

When We Say Thanks for Every Little Thing

* Beef Bourguignon with Gratin Dauphinoise
* Glazed Baby Carrots and Brussels Sprouts
* Red Velvet Cake with Cream Cheese Frosting

BEEF BOURGUIGNON

Makes 8 generous servings

* 6 slices thick bacon, coarsely chopped
* I tablespoon extra-virgin olive oil
* 3 pounds lean beef chuck roast, cut into 2-inch pieces
* I EACH: carrot and yellow onion, cut into thick slices
* Sea salt and freshly milled black pepper to taste
* 2 tablespoons all-purpose flour
* 3 cups full-bodied red wine, such as a pinot noir
* 3 cups brown beef stock
* I tablespoon tomato paste
* 2 cloves garlic, mashed
* I crumbled bay leaf
* 24 small white onions
* I pound quartered fresh brown mushrooms
* ½ cup all-purpose flour
* Parsley sprigs

– Preheat oven to 450°F.

– In a large heavy Dutch oven, sauté the bacon in oil over moderate heat for

2 to 3 minutes to brown lightly. Remove to a large side dish. Reheat the pot until fat is almost smoking before you sauté the beef.

– Dry the beef on paper towels. Sauté it, a few pieces at a time, in the hot oil and bacon fat until nicely browned on all sides. Add it to the bacon.

– In the same fat, brown the sliced vegetables. Pour out the sautéing fat.

– Return the beef and bacon to the Dutch oven and toss with the salt and pepper. Then sprinkle on the flour and toss again to coat the beef lightly with the flour. Set the pot uncovered in the middle position of a preheated oven for 4 minutes. Toss the meat and return to oven for 4 minutes more. (This browns the flour and covers the meat with a light crust.) Remove the Dutch oven, and turn the oven down to 325°F.

– Stir in the wine and stock so the meat is barely covered. Add the tomato paste, garlic, herbs, and bacon. Bring to simmer on top of the stove. Then cover the pot and set it in the lower third of the preheated oven. Bake slowly for 2½ to 3 hours, or until the meat is done when pierced with a fork easily.

– While the beef is cooking, prepare the onions and mushrooms. Toss each in flour, then braise in butter in a skillet. Set them aside until needed.

– When the meat is tender, distribute the cooked onions and mushrooms over the meat.

– Simmer sauce for a minute or two, skimming off additional fat as it rises. You should have about 2½ cups of sauce thick enough to coat a spoon lightly. If too thin, boil it down rapidly. If too thick, mix in a few tablespoons of stock, taste, and adjust seasoning. Pour the sauce over the meat and vegetables. Recipe may be completed in advance to this point.

– **For immediate serving:** Cover the Dutch oven and simmer for 2 to 3 minutes, basting the meat and vegetables with the sauce several times. Arrange the stew on a platter surrounded with potatoes and decorated with parsley. Transfer sauce to a gravy boat and serve on the side.

GRATIN DAUPHINOISE

Classic French cooking: this can be made ahead and reheated at serving time to accompany the beef. POW!

* 3 pounds Yukon gold potatoes (about 6 large)
* 1 medium leek
* ¾ teaspoon freshly ground white pepper
* ¼ teaspoon freshly grated nutmeg
* 2 tablespoons unsalted butter
* 1 large garlic clove, minced
* 2 cups whole milk
* ½ cup heavy creamy all at

– Preheat oven to 350°F with a rack in upper third of oven.

– Peel potatoes and thinly cut into ⅛-inch-thick slices, using a mandoline.

- Discard dark green part of leek and halve white and light green part lengthwise. Rinse layers under running water to remove any dirt and grit and pat dry. Thinly slice crosswise.

- Stir together white pepper and nutmeg with 1-¾ teaspoons salt in a small bowl. Melt butter in a small heavy saucepan over medium-low heat and cook leek and garlic, stirring frequently until softened, 3 to 5 minutes.

- Spread leek and butter mixture evenly in bottom of baking dish. Arrange one-quarter of the potatoes in a slightly overlapping layer over leeks. Pour ½ cup milk over potatoes, and sprinkle lightly with ½ teaspoon salt mixture. Layer potatoes with milk and salt mixture three more times in same manner.

- Place dish on a shallow baking pan and cover with foil. Bake until potatoes are almost tender, about 1 hour.

- Remove foil and pour cream over potatoes. Continue to bake, uncovered, until cream has been absorbed by potatoes and the top is golden in spots, 30 to 40 minutes.

GLAZED BABY CARROTS AND BRUSSELS SPROUTS

Makes 6 to 8 servings

* I pound baby carrots
* I pound Brussels sprouts, trimmed and scored
* I½ cups chicken broth
* 6 tablespoons butter
* ⅓ cup packed brown sugar

- Freshly milled black pepper and sea salt to taste

- Blanch carrots and Brussels sprouts in a large pot of boiling salted water until crisp-tender, about 4 minutes. Transfer to a bowl of ice water using slotted spoon.

- Bring stock, butter, and brown sugar to a boil in a heavy large skillet. Stir until sugar dissolves. Boil until reduced by half, about 7 minutes. Add carrots and Brussels sprouts. Cook until almost tender and sauce begins to coat, shaking pan occasionally, about 6 minutes. Add pepper and salt. Cook until heated through, stirring occasionally, about 4 minutes.

RED VELVET CAKE WITH CREAM CHEESE FROSTING

Makes 8 to 10 servings

* 2 ½ cups cake flour
* I ½ cup granulated sugar
* I teaspoon baking soda
* I teaspoon sea salt
* I teaspoon cocoa powder
* I ½ cups vegetable oil
* I cup buttermilk, at room temperature
* 2 large eggs, at room temperature
* 2 tablespoon red food coloring (I ounce)
* I teaspoon, white distilled vinegar
* I teaspoon vanilla extract

- Preheat the oven to 350 degrees F. Lightly

oil two 9 in round cake pans.

- In a large bowl, sift together the flour, sugar, baking soda, salt and cocoa powder. In another large bowl, whisk together the oil, buttermilk, eggs, food coloring, vinegar and vanilla.

- Using a mixer, mix the dry ingredients into the wet ingredients, until smooth.

- Pour batter into 2 greased 9 inch cake pans. Bake about 30 minutes or until the top of your finger does not leave an indentation, or insert toothpick in the center of the cake and it comes out clean.

- Cool on rack at least 20 minutes before turning it out onto a cake plate. Then ready to frost.

CREAM CHEESE FROSTING

* 1 (8 oz) cream cheese (softened)
* ½ cup butter (softened)
* 1 (1 pound) powdered sugar
* 1 ½ teaspoon vanilla extract
* 1 cup chopped pecans

- Beat cream cheese and butter until creamy; gradually add sugar and vanilla, beating well. Stir in pecans, Yield 3 cups

A Sandwich a Day

* Croque Monseius and Madame Sandwiches
* Curly Endive Salad with a Grapefruit Vinaigrette
* French Apple Tart

CROQUE MONSIEUR AND MADAME SANDWICHES

* 8 slices crusty bread
* Dijon mustard or mayonnaise
* 8 ounces thinly sliced ham
* 6 ounces thinly sliced cheese (such as Emmental, Comté, or Swiss)
* 4 tablespoons butter
* 4 eggs, beaten in a pie pan (optional for Madame)

- Heat a large skillet filmed with butter. Spread mustard and/or mayo onto bread slices, then lay on ham and cheese. Add second layer of bread and toast in the hot skillet.

- For a Madame sandwich: After making the sandwich, dip into beaten egg, then place in butter-filmed skillet and toast. Cut sandwich in half and serve hot.

CURLY ENDIVE SALAD WITH A GRAPEFRUIT VINAIGRETTE

* I large head of curly endive, washed, dried, and torn into bite-size pieces
* ¾ cup grapefruit vinaigrette
* Kosher salt and freshly ground black pepper to taste

- Place the endive in a large salad bowl. Drizzle the vinaigrette over the greens and toss to coat.

- Season to taste with sea salt and pepper.

Vinaigrette:

* Juice of one large grapefruit + water to make ½ cup
* ¾ cup extra-virgin olive oil
* Sea salt and freshly milled black pepper to taste

– Whisk in a small bowl, then toss with endive in a large salad bowl.

FRENCH APPLE TART

Serves 6

Dough:
* 2½ cups all-purpose flour
* 3 tablespoons granulated sugar
* ½ teaspoon sea salt
* ½ cup EACH: cold, unsalted butter and shortening
* 4 tablespoons ice water

Apple filling:
* 4 Granny Smith apples, peeled and cored, seeds removed
* ½ cup granulated sugar
* 4 tablespoons (½ stick) cold unsalted butter

– Add the flour, granulated sugar, and salt to the bowl of a food processor. Pulse a few times to mix all ingredients, then add butter and shortening; pulse until small bits look like cornmeal. With the motor running, add ice water, and pulse just until the dough comes together into a ball (do not overmix).

– Pour the dough ball onto a floured board, knead a little, then wrap the dough ball in plastic and refrigerate for 1 hour.

– Preheat the oven to 375°F.

– Line a sheet pan with parchment paper. Use a rolling pin to roll the dough to the shape of your tart pan, about a 9-inch circle. Cut off excess dough. Transfer the dough circle to the sheet pan and refrigerate while you cut the apples.

– Slice the apples about ¼ inch thick. Remove the tart from refrigerator. Begin laying in the apple slices, overlapping apples around the pan until the dough is fully covered. Sprinkle with granulated sugar and dots of butter. Bake for 45 minutes or until glistening and golden. Cool on a rack about 15 minutes, then cut into wedges and serve warm with your favorite ice cream or jam. What a feast! POW!

Jollof Party Time

* Jollof Party Rice
* Carolina-style Chicken Lollipops
* Roast Cauliflower with Almonds
* Lemon Pound Cake

JOLLOF PARTY RICE

Originally from Nigeria, this recipe travelled to the Caribbean and laid claim to Jamaica. Americans love it. Some folks chop the incendiary scotch bonnet into the mix; others just lay the little time bomb on top of the cooking rice, then discard it at serving time.

Makes 8 servings

* 1 large red bell pepper, seeded and quartered
* 1 scotch bonnet pepper (depending on how hot you want it, you can mince it into the rice or just lay it on top and discard it before serving)
* 2 medium beefsteak tomatoes, quartered
* 1 tablespoon tomato paste (optional)
* 2 cloves garlic
* 1 piece fresh ginger (about the size of your thumb)
* 1 small yellow onion
* 4 tablespoons sunflower oil or palm oil
* 2 cups vegetable stock
* 2 cups dry basmati rice
* 2 teaspoons fresh thyme
* Sea salt to taste
* 4 cups water, divided
* Fresh chopped basil and cilantro for garnish (optional)

- In the food processor, blend the peppers, tomatoes, onion, ginger, and garlic with 1 cup of water to form a smooth mixture.

- Heat the oil in a large, heavy pot and add the mixture, along with seasoning. Add the remaining 3 cups of water and bring to a boil.

- Add the rice to the mixture, stirring well, and then lower the heat completely. Cook for about 30 minutes, making sure the rice doesn't stick to the bottom of the pot and stirring from time to time (you might have to add a tiny bit more water as you go along). You want all the water to be absorbed and the rice texture to be light and fluffy.

- Toss a little fresh basil and cilantro in at the end. Serve in a wide, large bowl.

CAROLINA-STYLE CHICKEN LOLLIPOPS

Makes 8-10 servings

Great for a party. Use wings or drumsticks. Either way, you get bright, fresh, delicious bites that just scream FEAST. POW!

* 60 chicken wings (about 5 pounds) or 20 drumsticks
* 1 teaspoon EACH: kosher salt, smoked paprika, granulated garlic, granulated onion, and crushed red pepper
* 1 tablespoon brown sugar
* ½ cup apple cider vinegar

- With a paring knife, cut around the thin tip of each chicken wing to loosen the meat around the joint. While holding the base, push the meat down gently to expose the bone and form a "chicken lollipop." Remove any flesh left on the thin end with a clean towel.

- Combine dry ingredients with vinegar in a mixing bowl. Toss and cover. Store overnight in the refrigerator.

- Next day, preheat the oven to 350°F. Place chicken lollipops on a baking pan, standing up. Roast for 20 to 25 minutes. Serve immediately with your favorite barbecue sauce or Chef Jesse's honey BBQ sauce to give it a kick. POW!

ROASTED CAULIFLOWER WITH ALMONDS

Makes 6 servings

This recipe is so quick and easy, and very healthy.

* 3 tablespoons grape-seed oil
* 2 tablespoons Chef Jesse's spice blend (see pp 26)
* 1 large head cauliflower, separated into florets
* 1 cup whole almonds (lightly toasted in a skillet)

- Preheat the oven to 450°F. Grease a 9 x 13 casserole dish with butter.

- In a medium bowl, add grape-seed oil and chef Jesse's essence. Mix with a whisk.

- Add the cauliflower and mix well to coat. Transfer cauliflower to the prepared baking dish. Bake for 25 minutes or until tender and golden. Add toasted almonds and serve. POW!

〉〉〉〈〈〈

LEMON POUND CAKE

Makes 12-16 servings

Such a useful cake. This keeps well and tastes bright and clean. We love it.

* I cup unsalted butter, softened
* 2 cups granulated sugar
* 5 large eggs
* 3 cups cake flour
* I teaspoon sea salt
* ½ teaspoon EACH: baking powder and baking soda
* ¾ cup whole milk
* Grated zest of 2 fresh lemons
* ⅓ cup fresh squeezed lemon juice

– Preheat the oven to 350°F.

– Cream together the butter and granulated sugar until light and fluffy, then add eggs, one at a time, mixing well each time.

– In a medium bowl, mix flour, salt, baking powder, and baking soda together. In a small bowl, add milk with lemon zest and juice. Then, with the mixer on low, add flour in three parts, alternately with milk mixture in two and ending with flour.

– Mix until smooth. Grease your favorite Bundt pan. Add batter and bake for 90 minutes. Let the cake cool on a rack for 15 minutes or so, then turn out onto a cake plate.

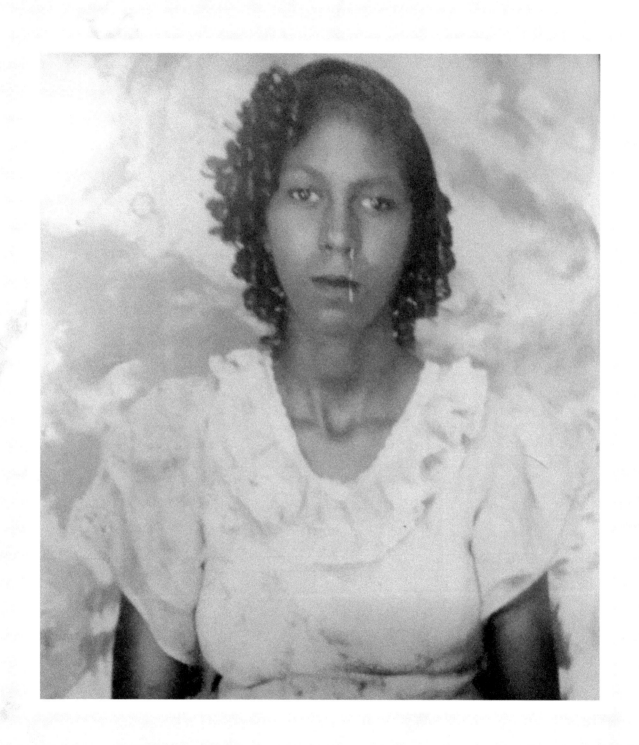

Thanksgiving

* My Mother-in Law's Alabama Queen Roast Turkey
* Corn Bread Sage Dressing
* Down-Home Candied Sweet Potatoes
* Collard Greens with Smoked Turkey Wings (SEE PAGE 70 FOR RECIPE)
* Mashed Potatoes and Giblet Gravy
* Turkey Stock
* Jellied Cranberry Sauce
* Molasses Cake (SEE PAGE i FOR RECIPE)

MY MOTHER-IN LAW'S ALABAMA QUEEN ROAST TURKEY

Makes 8 to 10 servings

For a real family reunion, when all the cousins and kids and aunts and uncles come to your house, everybody brings something. You cook the turkey and make the sides that you can't live without.

* 9- to 12-pound turkey, washed and giblets removed

Brine for turkey: Day 1
* 1 gallon of cold water
* 1 cup kosher salt
* ½ garlic clove
* 1 sprig of thyme

– In a large container (plastic only), add salt to water with garlic and thyme. Submerge turkey in container and marinate overnight, covered, in a cool place.

Feast #37

Day 2

* ½ cup unsalted butter
* 1 tablespoon chopped rosemary needles
* 1 clove garlic, minced
* ⅓ cup kosher salt
* 1 teaspoon coarse black pepper
* 2 carrots, peeled and rough cut
* ½ cup EACH: celery and onions, rough cut

— Heat the oven to 350°F.

— Rinse the turkey well, then cream together softened butter, garlic, and rosemary. Rub under the skin, in the cavity, and all over the turkey. Place carrots, celery, and onions in the cavity. Set turkey in large pan. Roast 3 to 4 hours, or until an instant-read thermometer reads 145°F when placed in the thickest part of the thigh.

— Let the bird rest about a half hour, then transfer to a cutting board. Cut into serving pieces, including thin slices of breast. Cut the wings and legs and thighs apart and arrange on a serving platter. Garnish with parsley and/or cranberries.

For instant help on turkey day, you can always call the turkey talk help line.

Butterball Turkey Talk Line
(800) BUTTERBALL (800-288-8373)

Available November 1 through December 28, weekdays 8 a.m. to 8 p.m. CST; Saturday and Sunday, 8 a.m. to 6 p.m. CST; Thanksgiving Day, 6 a.m. to 6 p.m. CST; Nov. 24 to Dec. 25, weekdays, 8 a.m. to 6 p.m. CST.

CORN BREAD SAGE DRESSING

When I first met my mother-in-law (Annie Will Spann), I fell in love with her cooking. Everything she made was awesome, but her dressing stood out for me.

This is my rendition. RIP to Queen of Alabama cooking. Your life is remembered with your fabulous recipes. Thank you.

Makes 6 servings

* ¼ cup vegetable oil
* 1 pound sage link breakfast sausage
* 1 small onion, peeled and finely diced
* 1 rib celery, finely diced
* 1 EACH: red and green pepper, seeded and finely diced
* ¼ cup fresh thyme, chopped
* 1 teaspoon poultry seasoning
* Chef Jesse's corn bread (recipe see page 70) or make your favorite in a black cast-iron skillet
* 1 cup turkey stock (recipe see page 192)
* 3 large eggs, beaten well
* ⅛ teaspoon cayenne pepper (or more to taste)

— Sea salt and freshly milled black pepper to taste

— In a large skillet, over high heat, add oil and sauté sausage for 2 minutes or until beginning to brown. Remove from the pan with a slotted spoon and set aside. In the same pan with drippings, sauté onion, celery, and peppers for 3 to 4 minutes or until onion begins to look clear and peppers begin to brown. Next add thyme and poultry seasoning. Stir to mix.

– In a large bowl, combine cornbread and sautéed vegetable mix with sausage, cayenne, salt and pepper to taste. Then add beaten eggs, mix lightly, and pour in first cup of the turkey stock. Mix well. You may need more stock. The mixture should be moist. Pour into greased 9 x 13 casserole dish, and bake for 45 minutes.

DOWN-HOME CANDIED SWEET POTATOES

Makes 8 servings

* 2 pounds sweet potatoes
* 1/2 cup (1 stick) unsalted butter
* 1/4 cup granulated sugar
* Pinch of sea salt
* 1 cup maple syrup
* 1/2 teaspoon cinnamon
* 1/2 teaspoon allspice
* 1/2 teaspoon pure vanilla extract

– Preheat the oven to 350°F. Bake the sweet potatoes until tender, but still a little firm, about 30 to 40 minutes. Set aside to cool. When cool, peel and cut into quarters.

– In a large skillet, melt the butter over medium heat, add granulated sugar, salt, maple syrup, cinnamon, allspice, and vanilla. Mix well. Add sweet potatoes to the sugar mix and place in a 9 x 13 casserole dish; bake for 15 minutes or until golden brown. Serve hot.

COLLARD GREENS WITH SMOKED TURKEY WINGS (SEE PAGE 70 FOR RECIPE)

MASHED POTATOES AND GIBLET GRAVY

Giblet Gravy
I learned this from the Queen of Alabama. Can't make a better dressing.

Serve it with your favorite mashed potatoes (SEE PAGE 30 FOR RECIPE). Pow!

Makes about 3 cups

* 1/4 cup grape-seed oil
* 1 carrot, medium dice
* 1 medium onion, medium dice
* 2 celery stalks, medium dice
* 1 garlic clove, crushed
* 2 sprigs of thyme
* 2 quarts water
* 1 chicken neck
* 1 chicken heart
* 1 chicken gizzard
* 1/8 teaspoon black pepper
* 1 teaspoon sea salt
* 1/4 cup butter
* 1/4 cup vegetable oil
* 1/2 cup all-purpose flour

– In a large Dutch oven or stockpot, add oil and heat over medium heat. Sauté carrots, onions, celery, and garlic for about 3 minutes. Add thyme and water, then add the neck, heart, and gizzard. Bring to boil and reduce heat, simmering until it reduces to 3 cups. Remove the giblets to cool. Finely dice them and set them aside.

– Melt the butter and oil in a large skillet over medium-high heat. Add giblets and sauté them for 2 to 3 minutes. Stir in the flour to make a roux, and cook mixture until nut brown and fragrant, about 5 minutes. Stir in the stock, bring to a boil, and simmer until thick. Cook 10 minutes more, and correct seasonings with salt and pepper. Transfer to a gravy boat and pass at the table.

TURKEY STOCK

Carefully made stock is the basis for many a great dish. After you have lovingly made this stock, store it covered in the refrigerator. Keeps 2 weeks, or 2 years in the freezer.

Makes 10 cups

* 3 pounds fresh turkey wings
* ¼ cup grape-seed oil
* 2 cups chopped onion
* 1 cup EACH: finely chopped carrots and celery
* 2 quarts cold water
* 4 sprigs EACH: fresh parsley and thyme
* 2 garlic cloves, smashed
* 2 teaspoons kosher salt (or to taste)
* ¼ teaspoon whole black peppercorns
* 1 bay leaf

– Preheat oven to 450°F.

– Chop turkey wings with a cleaver or have your butcher cut them in ½ inch pieces. place in a roasting pan then roast wings for 30 minutes, turning them to brown evenly.

– In a medium stock pot, heat oil, then cook onions, carrots and celery until soft, about 10 minutes. Add the wings to the pot, deglaze the pan with water, scraping all the solids from the bottom, then add wings and cover with water. Bring to a high boil, skimming foam off, then add parsley, fresh thyme, garlic and salt. Add peppercorns and bay leaf, then reduce to low, and simmer, uncovered, for 3 hours, adding more water as needed to keep wings covered. Strain stock through a fine sieve, skim off excess fat, taste and adjust seasonings, then transfer to clean glass jars and store in the refrigerator.

JELLIED CRANBERRY SAUCE

Buy this in a can if you like the clear red sauce. Or make your own. Pow!

Makes 1 cup

* 1 cup granulated sugar
* 1 cup water
* 1 12-ounce package Ocean Spray fresh or frozen cranberries

Directions

– Combine granulated sugar and water in a medium saucepan. Bring to a boil and add cranberries. Return to a boil. Reduce heat and boil gently for 10 minutes, stirring occasionally.

– Place a wire mesh strainer over a medium mixing bowl. Pour contents of saucepan into strainer. Mash cranberries with the back of a spoon, frequently scraping the outside of the strainer until no pulp is left.

- Stir contents of bowl. Pour into serving container. Cover and cool completely at room temperature. Refrigerate until serving time.

MOLASSES CAKE (SEE PAGE i FOR RECIPE)

Chapter 12: December

The Blowout Christmas Parties to Blast Off the Season

CHEF JESSE'S COQ AU VIN

Makes 6 servings

Julia Child first brought this dish to American cooks in the sixties via her popular cooking show. There have been many versions. Here's mine.

＊ 6 chicken legs, washed

＊ 4 ounces thick, smoked bacon cut into rectangles

＊ 2 tablespoons olive oil

＊ I teaspoon Chef Jesse's spice blend (see pp 26)

＊ ¼ cup cognac

＊ 2 cups red wine (pinot noir or burgundy)

＊ 2 cups homemade chicken stock (or low-sodium canned chicken stock)

＊ I tablespoon tomato paste

＊ 2 cloves garlic, smashed

＊ I bay leaf

＊ 4 sprigs fresh thyme

＊ 12 boiler onions or pearl onions (see recipe below for browned, braised onions)

Feast #38

* ½ pound white medium mushrooms (see recipe below)
* 3 tablespoons all-purpose flour
* 2 tablespoons butter, softened

Browned, Braised Onion Recipe:
* 12 small boiler onions
* 1-2 tablespoons olive oil
* Sea salt to taste

- Heat oil in a medium saucepan over medium heat and add onions. Slow cook until browned. Add salt and ½ cup water. Simmer 25 minutes or until soft.

Mushroom Recipe:
* ½ pound white mushrooms, washed and sliced or quartered
* 1 tablespoon butter + ½ tablespoon olive oil

- In a large pan heat butter and olive oil. When hot, add mushrooms and slow cook until brown, about 4-5 minutes. Set aside.

To Make the Coq au Vin:
Dry chicken legs in a towel to assure crispy searing. Season with Chef Jesse's spice blend.
- Cook bacon in the bottom of a Dutch oven until crisp. Remove the bacon to a side dish. In the same pan, sear chicken legs on all sides until fully browned. Pour in the cognac and flambé by lighting with a match, burning off the alcohol. Pour in the red wine and chicken stock, just enough to cover the chicken legs. Stir in tomato paste, garlic, bay leaf, and thyme. Bring the liquid to a simmer, then cover the pot. Place in a 300°F oven for 45 minutes or until fork tender. When chicken legs are finished, remove them onto a platter. Bring cooking

liquid to a simmer on the stovetop. In a small bowl, blend the 3 tablespoons flour and 2 tablespoons soft butter into a smooth paste. Add to liquid while stirring constantly to prevent lumps. Cook for a few more minutes. Mix in mushrooms, braised onions, bacon, and chicken. Serve hot.

GREEN BEAN CASSEROLE

Serves 6 to 8

* 1½ pounds fresh green beans, snipped on both ends
* ½ cup unsalted butter
* 1 small yellow onion, peeled and chopped
* 2 tablespoons all-purpose flour
* 1 cup half-and-half
* 1 cup Boursin cheese
* 1 cup sharp cheddar cheese
* 1 cup panko bread crumbs

- Bring a large pot of salted water to a boil, add beans, and cook until tender, about 5 minutes. Drain, then transfer to an ice water bath. Let cool for few minutes, then drain again and reserve.

- Melt butter in a medium skillet, add onions, and sauté for 2 minutes. Add flour to make a roux. Cook for a few minutes until onions are golden, then slowly add half-and-half and cook until it thickens. Add Boursin cheese and simmer for a few minutes. Adjust seasonings to taste with salt and pepper.

- In a medium bowl, add beans, then pour cheese mixture over the beans, mix well, and transfer to a casserole dish. Sprinkle with cheddar cheese and panko bread crumbs. Bake in a 400°F oven for 20 minutes. Serve hot.

POTATOES LYONNAISE

Makes 6 servings

* 2 tablespoons grape-seed oil
* 2 pounds Idaho potatoes, peeled and sliced about ¼-inch thick
* Kosher salt and freshly milled black pepper to taste
* 4 tablespoons unsalted butter
* 3 large yellow onions, peeled and cut julienne (into thin strips)
* 2 tablespoons EACH: minced garlic and parsley

— Heat oil in a Dutch oven over medium-low heat. Add 1 layer of potatoes to start the browning process. Season with salt and pepper. Add butter, onions, and garlic. Keep adding layers until they're all in the pan. Cook 10 to 15 minutes, turning and browning, slowly. When the dish is fork tender, pour onto a platter and garnish with parsley to serve.

ORANGE WALNUT BUNDT CAKE

(Yield -10 inch)

* 2 cups cake flour
* 1 teaspoon baking power
* ½ teaspoon baking soda

* Pinch of sea salt
* ½ pound unsalted butter, softened
* 1 ½ cups sugar
* 3 large eggs
* 1 cup orange juice
* 1 teaspoon vanilla extract
* 1 cup chopped walnuts
* 1 tablespoon grated orange zest

— Preheat heat oven 350 degrees F. Butter and flour a ten-inch Bundt pan.

— Sift flour, baking powder, and salt together and sit aside. In a mixer cream the butter and sugar together until light. Then beat in eggs one at a time. Add the flour alternately with one cup of the orange juice and the vanilla. Fold in the orange zest and walnuts.

— Pour cake batter into greased ten-inch Bundt pan. Bake in oven 1 hour or until brown and toothpick comes out clean.

— Cool on rack for about an hour, and then turn onto a cake platter.

Hunters' Lunch

* Chef Jesse's Venison Chili

* Cheesy Biscuits (See recipe page 74)

* Simple Marinated Cucumbers with Cider Vinaigrette

* One-Bowl Yellow Cake with a Limoncello Infusion

CHEF JESSE'S VENISON CHILI

If you are a hunter, you'll be glad for this great way to cook your catch. Those of you who hunt in specialty grocery stores can purchase venison in specialty stores or online.

I came to love venison working under the great chefs at Dennis Foy's Town Square in Chatham, New Jersey. So flavorful and yet so lean. I buy it from Fossil Farms in Boonton, New Jersey.

* I teaspoon grape-seed oil
* 4 pounds ground venison
* I cup chopped yellow onions
* ½ cup fresh red peppers
* ½ cup fresh green peppers
* 4 cloves garlic, chopped
* I tablespoon, chopped canned chipotle, in adobo sauce
* 3 tablespoons ground cumin
* 3 tablespoons ground chili powder
* I cup tomato puree
* 2 cups water
* I cup diced fresh plum tomatoes
* I cup EACH: dried pinto beans and black beans*
* 4 ounces bittersweet chocolate

- In a heavy sauce pot, heat grape-seed oil to medium and sauté the ground venison until brown. Place in a strainer to discard any fat, then set aside.

- In the same pot, add a little oil, and sauté onions, peppers, garlic, and chipotle pepper, for 3 minutes. Add cumin, chili powder, and tomato puree. Let the flavors mellow together, about 10 minutes.

- Add fresh diced tomatoes and cooked beans with venison and let it cook for about 30 minutes. Add chocolate and adjust favors.

- *Start with dried beans by soaking them overnight in water to cover. You can cook them together in a pot of barely boiling water until tender, about 1 hour. OR you can start with canned beans. Simply strain and add to the pot.

SIMPLE MARINATED CUCUMBERS WITH CIDER VINAIGRETTE

* 2 English cucumbers, peeled and sliced thin
* I cup cider vinegar
* ½ cup water
* I tablespoon EACH: granulated sugar, salt, seeded mustard
* Freshly milled black pepper to taste

- Place cucumbers in a bowl. Combine remaining ingredients in a small bowl. Whisk and pour over the cucumbers. Cover and refrigerate (keeps up to a week).

ONE-BOWL YELLOW LAYER CAKE WITH A LIMONCELLO INFUSION

This recipe is more than 100 years old, but once I started giving it little sips of limoncello, it began to sing. POW!

* 2 cups all-purpose flour, spooned and leveled; sifted after measuring
* I + ¼ cup granulated sugar
* I tablespoon baking powder
* I teaspoon salt
* ½ cup butter, softened
* I cup milk
* I teaspoon vanilla extract
* 2 eggs

Whipped Cream Frosting
* I cup heavy whipping cream
* ½ teaspoon pure vanilla extract
* I tablespoon granulated sugar

Limoncello Infusion
* 2 tablespoons limoncello liqueur

- Preheat oven to 350°F. Grease and flour two 8-inch cake pans.

- In a large mixing bowl, sift together flour, granulated sugar, baking powder, and salt.

- Add butter, milk, and vanilla. Beat with a hand mixer on medium speed for 3-4 minutes, occasionally scraping sides of bowl. Add eggs and beat for 3 more minutes.

- Pour batter into prepared pans, dividing equally among both. Bake 30 to 35 minutes or until toothpick comes out clean.

- Cool in pans on wire racks 10 minutes. Turn out and cool thoroughly on wire racks. Add sips of limoncello to cake layers as they cool.

- Frost with whipped cream frosting. Refrigerate until serving time.

Whipped Cream Frosting:

- Combine all ingredients in a large mixing bowl; cover and chill in refrigerator 30 minutes with the beaters.

- Beat on medium speed until stiff peaks form. Frost sides and top of the cake.

Christmas Eve Family Dinner

* Pineapple-Spiked and Apple-Glazed Whole Ham

* Roasted Winter Roots, including parsnips,
carrots, sweet potatoes, andwinter squash

* Christmas Salad with Baby Kale and Dried Cranberries

* Three Cheese Baken Macaroni

* Hummingbird Cake (SEE PAGE 122 FOR RECIPE)

My Aunt Mitt (aka Aunt Bull) is the pork queen, but what makes her hams so good is that she is picky and only uses a fresh, uncured ham. Plus, she takes her time, never skipping any steps. Thanks, Aunty, for all the inspiration.

This is an example of the care taken in my family to make wonderful meals worthy of a celebration as our own family Christmas Eve dinner.

In some families, the presents are the main emphasis. In our family, it's always been all about the food.

PINEAPPLE-SPIKED AND APPLE-GLAZED WHOLE HAM

Makes 12 to 15 servings

* 1 whole fresh ham (bone-in, uncured, 10 to 15 pounds)
* 1 tablespoon grape-seed oil
* 1 ½ cups Chef Jesse's Spice Blend (see pp 26)
* 1 tablespoon rendered fat from the ham
* 1 whole fresh pineapple (peeled, cored, and diced)
* 3 Granny Smith apples (peeled, cored, and diced)
* 1 cup apple juice

* ½ cup EACH: bourbon, brown sugar, maple syrup, and apple cider vinegar
* 1 teaspoon crushed red pepper
* 2 teaspoons ground cloves

- In a medium bowl, combine grape-seed oil and Chef Jesse's spice blend. Mix well, and coat the ham on all sides. Marinate overnight, covered in the refrigerator.

Next day:

- Preheat oven to 325°F.

- In a roasting pan with a rack, add the ham and roast for 4 hours, uncovered, or until an internal temperature of 160°F is reached. Cool on a rack at least 2 hours.

- About two hours in, make this sauce and brush half of it over the ham for glaze:

- In a medium saucepan, add 2 tablespoons rendered ham fat and sauté the pineapple and apples for 5 minutes, or until sweated down. Add the bourbon and cook for 1 minute. Add the apple juice, brown sugar, and maple syrup. Cook and stir for 10 minutes, adjust the seasoning, and remove from the heat.

- When cool, take ½ the sauce out to a bowl and puree with the stick blender, but leave the rest whole. Add the pureed sauce into the chopped mix.

- With about 1 hour left in roasting time, brush some of the glaze over the ham and then finish roasting time, reserving the rest to serve over ham.

- Let the ham rest for about 20 minutes before carving.

ROASTED WINTER ROOTS, INCLUDING PARSNIPS, CARROTS, SWEET POTATOES, AND WINTER SQUASH

This is a wonderful, very easy side dish that you will love to make even as a snack.

Makes 8 servings

* 1 pound EACH: parsnips and carrots, peeled and cut into 1¼-inch pieces
* 1 large, sweet potato, peeled and cut into 1¼-inch pieces
* 2 pounds butternut squash, peeled and cut into 1¼-inch pieces
* ¼ cup grape-seed oil
* 3 sprigs of fresh thyme
* Sea salt and freshly ground pepper, to taste

- Preheat oven to 375°F.

- Heat the oil in large roasting pan in a hot oven and add vegetables. Toss in the oil and season to taste with sea salt, freshly ground black pepper, and thyme. Roast for 1½ hours. Every few minutes, give it a stir. Adjust seasonings and then transfer into your favorite serving vessel. Great hot or room temp. POW!

CHRISTMAS SALAD WITH BABY KALE AND DRIED CRANBERRIES

Makes 6-8 servings

This is a wonderful, quick salad to make for Christmas. It goes perfectly with the fresh ham. But the kicker is my apple-cider vinaigrette, which I use over and over. I try to make up a batch and keep it in the refrigerator. It makes any salad go POW!

* 4 cups baby kale, washed, spun dried, and torn into bite-sized pieces
* I cup sweetened dried cranberries

Apple Cider Vinaigrette:
* ½ teaspoon Dijon mustard
* I teaspoon EACH: fresh minced thyme, chopped shallots, hot sauce, maple syrup, and kosher salt
* 3 tablespoons EACH: apple cider vinegar and apple juice
* I½ cups grape-seed oil
* Few cranks of fresh black pepper

– In a salad bowl, toss the baby kale and dried cranberries.

To make the vinaigrette:
– In a blender, combine mustard, thyme, shallots, maple syrup, salt, apple cider vinegar, and apple juice. Pulse once and then with the blender running, slowly pour in grape-seed oil until mixture is thick. Adjust the taste and finish with cracked pepper.

– Transfer to a covered jar and refrigerate until serving time.

– Arrange baby kale and dried cranberries in a nice bowl, then just before service, toss with vinaigrette and serve. POW!

THREE CHEESE BAKED MACARONI

Makes 8 to 10 servings

* I teaspoon sea salt
* 2 cups elbow macaroni, cooked following package directions
* ½ stick butter
* ½ cup all-purpose flour
* 4 cups evaporated milk
* I teaspoon kosher salt
* ½ teaspoon cayenne pepper
* Pinch white pepper
* 2 cups EACH: shredded white extra sharp and mild cheddar
* I cup Colby cheese, grated
* (mix cheeses and blend together)
* 2 large eggs, beaten
* Sprinkling of paprika

– Preheat oven to 350 F.

– In a large heavy-duty pot, melt butter, then add flour, to make a roux, then add milk, stir until smooth with no lumps, then add salt, cayenne, white pepper, and ½ of the cheese blend. Save remainder for topping later.   Melt, then turn off the heat. In a large mixing bowl, add cooked macaroni, cheese sauce, taste for salt, then add 2 beaten eggs, mix well. Pour into a buttered 2 quart casserole dish, sprinkle with saved cheese and paprika, bake uncovered, until golden brown 40 to 45 minutes.

December New Year's Eve

Bonus gift from me to you for a dazzling end to a splendid year.

Happy New Year to you and yours!

New Year's Eve Midnight Supper

* Roast Rack of Pork with Fig and Apple Chutney
* Potato Pancakes
* Green Broccoli Rabe with Garlic and Crushed Red Pepper
* Chef Jesse's Banana Tart with Maple Ice Cream

ROASTED RACK OF PORK WITH FIG AND APPLE CHUTNEY

Chef's Note: Serve this dish family-style on a great big platter, laced with the fig chutney.

Ask the butcher to cut and tie this wonderful festive dish. It will buckle your knees.

Makes 6 to 8 servings

* I rack of pork (normally about 3 pounds)
* ½ cup grape-seed oil
* I teaspoon minced garlic
* I teaspoon minced fresh rosemary
* I teaspoon minced thyme
* I teaspoon minced sage

- Combine the grape-seed oil, garlic, rosemary, thyme, sage, and pork in a glass dish. Rub pork in the mixture. Cover and refrigerate overnight.

Next Day:

- Take out the pork. Sear on all sides and then transfer to the oven. Roast at 325°F for approximately 1½ hours or to an internal temperature of 160°F. Let it rest on the sideboard at least 20 minutes before carving. POW!

FIG AND APPLE CHUTNEY

* 6 dried mission figs (use fresh if available)
* 2 tablespoons granulated sugar
* I cup ruby port
* ½ cup red wine vinegar
* 2 teaspoons mustard seed
* ½ teaspoon EACH: ground cinnamon and allspice
* 2 whole cloves
* ¼ teaspoon EACH: cayenne pepper and kosher salt
* I medium red onion
* 2½ pounds Granny Smith apples
* I teaspoon EACH: orange zest, lemon zest, and lemon juice

- Combine figs, sugar, port, vinegar, mustard seeds, cinnamon, allspice, cloves, cayenne pepper, and salt in a non-reactive pan. Bring to a boil on medium heat. Reduce about half 10 to 15 minutes, until the figs are tender. Stir in apples. Let simmer for 30 minutes. Transfer to a bowl.

- Serve hot or cold.

POTATO PANCAKES

Serves 8 to 12

* 4 medium baking potatoes (Idaho is my go-to potato), peeled
* I small yellow onion, peeled and chopped
* ¼ cup all-purpose flour
* I egg, beaten
* I teaspoon sea salt
* I teaspoon fresh thyme
* Few cranks of fresh cracked black pepper
* ¾ cup vegetable oil, for frying

- Shred potatoes and onion in a food processor or a box grater. Squeeze potatoes and onion between paper towels to remove all moisture, then transfer to a bowl. Stir in flour, salt, thyme, and pepper, until blended. In a large skillet heated over medium high heat and filmed with hot oil, place 2 tablespoons of potato mixture individually, and fry over medium high-heat, turning once, until golden brown. Drain on paper towels.

SEARED GREEN BROCCOLI RABE WITH GARLIC AND CRUSHED RED PEPPER

Makes 8 servings

* 2 bunches broccoli rabe, chopped
* ½ cup EACH: water and butter
* Sea salt and freshly milled black pepper to taste
* ½ teaspoon EACH: fresh crushed garlic and crushed red pepper

- Heat a large skillet over high heat. Add all

ingredients, stirring until the broccoli is wilted. Serve at once.

CHEF JESSE'S BANANA TART

One of my most requested desserts. I know you're gonna love it.

Makes 8 individual tarts

* ½ cup (I stick) butter
* I teaspoon ground cinnamon
* I cup packed dark brown sugar
* ½ cup banana liqueur
* 8 medium bananas, peeled, cut in slices

To Make Tart Dough:
* 5¼ cups pastry flour or all-purpose flour
* I tablespoon kosher salt
* 1½ cups cold unsalted butter, cut into small pieces
* 1¾ cups solid vegetable shortening, chilled
* I cup ice water

- Combine flour and salt into a bowl. Add the butter and shortening and mix until it resembles coarse meal. Add ice water to form dough. Wrap and place in refrigerator for 1 hour.

- In a large skillet, melt the butter. Add cinnamon and brown sugar and stir, simmering over medium heat until the sugar dissolves, 3 to 4 minutes. Add the banana liqueur and blend well. Add sliced bananas and cook for 6 minutes. Cool.

- Roll pastry out on a lightly floured work surface and line the tart tin. Prick the

pastry base, and put cooked bananas over pastry. Bake for 30-40 minutes at 350°F.

MAPLE ICE CREAM

Yields 2 quarts

* 1½ cups heavy whipping cream
* 1½ cups half-and-half
* 6 large egg yolks
* I cup maple syrup
* ¼ teaspoon sea salt
* I tablespoon vanilla extract

- Bring heavy cream and half-and-half to simmer in heavy, large saucepan over medium-high heat. Remove from heat.

- Combine eggs yolks, maple syrup, and sea salt in a large bowl; whisk until thick and blended. Gradually whisk hot cream mixture into yolk mixture. Return mixture to same saucepan and stir over medium-low heat until custard thickens, about 3 minutes. Remove from heat and mix in vanilla extract. Refrigerate custard, uncovered, until cold. Stirring occasionally, add to ice cream machine. Freeze, then remove the paddle from the canister. Place ice cream in the freezer until ready to serve.

End note:

How I Found My Spot

And My Place in the World.

Faith riders, mount up. Let's get it. POW! Dream big, never give up; that's my redemption now!

It's what I pray for every morning of my life. I say it like a chant, over and over as I walk into the park in the morning and head to the path, taking long, sure steps.

That takes me to my spot, deep in the leafy green arms of the park.

It's what I say after I've parked the car and walked over the crunchy gravel to get to the path that takes me to my spot. And I learned to say this prayer when I found my spot.

But before all of that, let me explain. I have a special park bench I call MY SPOT, located in South Orange, New Jersey, my hometown. I started going there when everything in my life seemed to turn against me. I had lost my restaurant, my home, and my self-respect. I couldn't even look myself in the mirror. I was paralyzed with fear.

I found my spot when I walked in the park because I couldn't face looking my folks in the face. When things got impossibly hard, I just started going to my spot, and now, I go there every morning to start my day. All I could do at first was slam that car door, take a few gulps of the crisp morning air, and start walking.

This is where I go to ask God questions.

"Dear Lord, what do I do now? I have lost everything."

Sometimes I just ask, "Why did you wake me up this morning? I'm a complete failure. I cannot go on."

But the miracle is this. Through planting my seat on that park bench morning after morning, in good weather and bad, in happy days and fearful ones, year after year, I have learned that my spot is special. When I go and talk to God, things happen.

Maybe I'll get a call for a job, or several jobs. And sometimes, I just get calls from people telling me how they appreciate me and how they enjoyed my food and how I have lifted them up. Sometimes people tell me how my meal made their family feel.

The one thing I know for sure is that I have to be really still, sitting on that bench, with only the birds in the trees and the wind in the leaves saying anything besides whatever it is that God is telling me on that day. I have to open up my heart and listen hard.

But this much I can tell you, my spot really changed my perspective on life. I do believe it is God talking to me, as well as my grandmother and everyone else I lost along the way, who are outstretching their hands to help me. I know I could never do this alone. Never.

Now, when I go to my spot, I just tell God, "Thank you for waking me up. I will continue to love my family, to help the sick and the homeless. I will be humble and kind." I know we often ask God for things, but we sometimes forget we need to be thankful.

I'm blessed to be alive. Every day, when I go to my spot, I say thank God. Thank you to those who have gone before me: Grandmother, everyone, and now Zeus; for everything and for everyone who is praying for me, I give thanks. POW!

Index

CPSIA information can be obtained
at www.ICGtesting.com
Printed in the USA
LVHW07*1446140818
586953LV00023B/357/P